Hydroponics

The Beginner's Guide to Learning The DIY Techniques to Start Growing Organic Vegetables and Design Your Sustainable Garden Without Soil at Home.

Andy Anson

TABLE OF CONTENTS

INTRODUCTION
What Is Hydroponics?

Hydroponics is the art of growing plants without using soil. To do this, hydroponics devices typically include a storage tank that has nutrients and some kind of gadget that lugs this nutrient solution to the plants.

Garden enthusiasts can make use of a range of different growth mediums in which to place the plants. As opposed to using dirt, as an example, lots of gardeners will certainly utilize rockwool, gravel, sand, or perhaps coco coir. Unlike dirt, which supplies nutrients to the roots of plants, these growth tools simply supply room and also assistance for the roots to expand. Because of that, these mediums require to be inert.

Hydroponics is preferred since it has several one-of-a-kind advantages for the gardener. Primarily, it conserves money by permitting the garden enthusiast to reuse any type of water that is made use of. And, considering that the nutrients are absorbed more effectively, as well as controlled completely by the gardener, the expense of plant food is vastly reduced. On top of that, the yields of plants expanded in hydroponics are steady as well as usually fairly high.

Probably the very best advantage of hydroponics is the truth that it can be grown indoors, which suggests that your horticulture is no longer restricted by the period in which you choose to grow it. So, also in the middle of the winter season, you can grow plants that are healthy and solid.

Why do plants grown with hydroponics grow faster than plants that don't use it?

Basically, hydroponics gives the plant specifically what it requires when it needs it. This means that your plants can expand at the fastest speed that their genes enable. When contrasted to a plant grown in a requirement, soil-based atmosphere, hydroponically expanded plants expand at a much faster rate, and also typically appear healthier.

Just how challenging is it to use hydroponics equipment?

The effectiveness of hydroponics tools depends upon the ability of the garden enthusiast. If you can locate the correct pH, growing tool, and also innovation, you could be astonished at the outcomes. That being claimed, hydroponics devices are not necessarily tough to use. Basic knowledge of the tools, integrated with a little scientific knowledge, will suffice to satisfy any kind of garden enthusiast. These details can easily be located online.

Nevertheless, if you do intend to understand it, you will certainly need to have a look at a few of the more advanced resources of details, like books as well as toolsets. For some individuals, obtaining the understanding to grow the best plants utilizing hydroponics is one of the most exciting parts of horticulture.

Who Invented Hydroponics?

Many people mistakenly believe that the art of growing plants successfully without using soil, known as hydroponics, is a new technology. Leading Hydroponics experts and suppliers, Great Stuff Hydroponics, aim to throw some light on the origins of this ancient technique.

It is commonly thought amongst gardening experts that the famous hanging gardens of Babylon could be the earliest example of a complex use of hydroponic techniques. Freshwater containing plenty of oxygen and nutrients were used to keep plants alive without having any soil surrounding their root structures. Other possible uses of hydroponics in the ancient world have also been suggested within Aztec culture.

However, it was not until the middle ages when scientific knowledge about the workings of plant life began to develop. In 1600, Jan Van Helmont deduced that plants take their nutrients only from the rainwater, rather than from the soil itself.

He realized this because plant mass rises according to plant growth over time; however, soil mass stays much the same. This paved the way for scientists and chemists to find out more about exactly which nutrients need to be present in water to promote healthy plant growth.

Then the English scientist, Joseph Priestly, discovered that plants photosynthesize, converting carbon dioxide into oxygen, and that this process is speeded up when the plant is exposed to bright sunlight. This was also an important development regarding the lighting techniques which are now used for commercial hydroponic growth.

By the mid-1800s as a result of much interest in the subject and many experiments, a definitive list of minerals and nutrients needed by plants in order to thrive had been developed, with nutrient solutions created by the German botanist Wilhelm Knop.

The techniques of hydroponic growth, such as controlling the amount of light, water, and nutrients available to the plant, are ideally suited to growing plants indoors. For this reason, in the first half of the twentieth century, commercial greenhouse growers began to realize the potential of hydroponics.

Hydroponic plant growth uses only 1/20th of the water that traditional (soil-based) agriculture demands. Also, soil-borne diseases and virtually all pests are eliminated.

These growth techniques are not only environmentally friendly, using less water and reducing agricultural 'run-off,' which would normally find its way into the water table, but it is also ideally suited to arid climates. This was proven brilliantly during the war, when American troops stationed on barren Wake Island in the Pacific, were able to survive by growing fresh food hydroponically.

Dr. William Gericke perfected hydroponic techniques during the 1940s, and even decided upon the name for them, amalgamating the Greek 'hydros' (meaning 'water') and 'ponos' (which means 'working') into one word.

Since then, hydroponic growth techniques have diversified into a variety of ways to grow plants in 'soil-less cultures,' although they use other media instead of soil, which means that not all soil-less cultures can strictly be defined as hydroponic any more. Not only that, but there is now also a plethora of different growth promoters, nutrient solutions, and hydroponic lighting designed for different aspects of plant growth on the market.

No single person or culture developed hydroponics; however, the broad depth of modern scientific knowledge on the subject, drawn from many developments and experiments over time, mean that it is a viable commercial agricultural method and is also well suited to researchers, hobbyists, and enthusiasts alike. Amazingly, this ancient technique can be practiced at home, using one of the hydroponic kits available online from Great Stuff Hydroponics. Kits can be supplied to beginners and advanced growers in addition to all other hydroponic equipment and specialist supplies.

EVOLUTION OF HYDROPONICS

If you inquire, our concepts in modern hydroponics differ significantly. But for other people, they think of hydroponics as a new science (probably due in part to NASA's usage of it in space testing). However, the fact is that hydroponics is not a new player in the league. Yeah, from the very dawn of hydroponics, we have achieved a lot of progress, but that is typically over thousands of years. In order to better understand the legacy of our current hydroponics, we can look at the hydroponics past. Briefly, at least, it's got roots in ancient legends.

The mythical hanging gardens in Babylon, which was built by King Nebuchadnezzar II as a treat for his wife Amytis, is reported to have existed about 500 B.C.E.

The complex irrigation structures that sustain the large gardens have long been researched by academics and archeologists. With sophisticated stones that carry trees, a steady supply from central water reservoirs supplied water. The plants were fed and aerated by the constant flow of water to their roots.

Greek historians have described the legendary gardens saying:

"Water streams from high reservoirs pass on inclined channels. The waters irrigate the entire garden and saturate the plant roots and keep the whole field damp. The lawn is thus green forever, and the leaves of the trees are tightly bound to versatile roots."

Although we can suggest that these hanging gardens are the material of folklore without a reliable archeological finding, historians have been well known. And the following quote is a relatively simple explanation of hydroponic practices but for the beginner hydroponic gardener.

The Ancient Far East

It has been rising hydroponically for about as long as rice has been a crop grown in Asia. The picture you possibly conjure up in your head is the vast rice paddies across China. To be honest, this is a reasonably objective measurement.

Factors like size, distance, processing, and other small specifics might have improved, but there isn't much. The critical method of rice cultivation is the same.

At the very beginning of rice development, attempts were made to cultivate rice in soil. While it was tighter, rice as a crop was a good investment. Many other food crops have been killed following major periodic floods. However, rice was not only immune to the watery circumstances, but it also prospered. This was the spark that shone the light in hydroponic rice farming until now. After the revelation, rice was cultivated deliberately in controlled water systems. The rice not only developed stronger but defied more diseases and pests than other crops as an additional advantage for hydroponic positioning.

We have more documents that have continued and expanded the usage of hydroponics in China. When Marco Polo documented his journeys in the 13th century, China only used hydroponics for rice farming as an esthetic pleasure. Polo mentioned "floating gardens" floating on platforms of water.

It should also be pointed out that while rice fields were used for hydroponic harvests, they often supported more diverse food sources. Today, we use the term 'aquaponics' in hydroponics where fish are still housed, often in agricultural conditions for fish growth. A similar program was developed in Indochina and China.

In the flooded rice paddy already in use for grain production, fish were raised and cultivated.

How does aquaponics work?

Modern aquaponics has the same ideas used in rice fields traditionally but with a bit more complexity and far more equipment. In principle, when a typical hydroponic system has a nutrient solution reservoir, an aquaponic system is fitted with a fish tank. A pump carries the water to the rising tray or the bed of the plant. Excess water is drained from the roots of the plant and added to the tank (making it healthy again for fish). The fish waste then fills the water with nutrients, which are then added to the above plants.

Hydroponics in the pyramids?

It is not so well known, but it is no less real. Archaeologists find written proof of this in documents documenting the practices and uses of certain early hydroponic practices that relied on the Nile. The ancient Egyptians used hydroponic methods as early as many centuries before B.C.E.

And, unfortunately, our dreams are not correct of hydroponic pyramids. But hieroglyphs were found that tells us the tale of an imaginative individual who uses the Nile River to plant soilless crops.

CHAPTER ONE

A BEGINNER'S GUIDE TO HYDROPONIC GARDENING

Hydroponics is a greenhouse that does not utilize fertilizer but instead cultivates plants in a water and nutrient solution. The first move to building up a hydroponic garden is to pick a device that fits the specifications best. Significant considerations are: how much space you have, how fast you need to expand, how much expense, and how much time you need to sustain the program.

Benefit of Hydroponic Gardening

Hydroponic planting has many advantages:

- Plants expand more rapidly. Experts say that plants in hydroponic systems expand at least 20 percent faster than in soil.
- The yields of hydroponic systems are 20 to 25 percent higher than in soil processing.
- There is no requirement for a soil that may provide a strong benefit in places where the current garden land is bad even for people who have little connection to the garden plot.
- Hydroponic cultivation requires less space.
  The plants will not have to develop broad root systems to provide the nutrients that they require in order to bundle them tightly together— another benefit for those who have to garden indoors.

Water has been preserved. The hydroponic tanks are capped, and the structures are enclosed to avoid evaporation. This makes it easier for plants only to take the water they need.

3 Hydroponic Garden Setups for Beginners

For newcomers, the three most common settings are wicked, water culture, and ebb and flow. The three can be made from single pieces that have been ordered separately, or a full set-up package can be bought from online suppliers or hydroponic stores.

Wick Systems

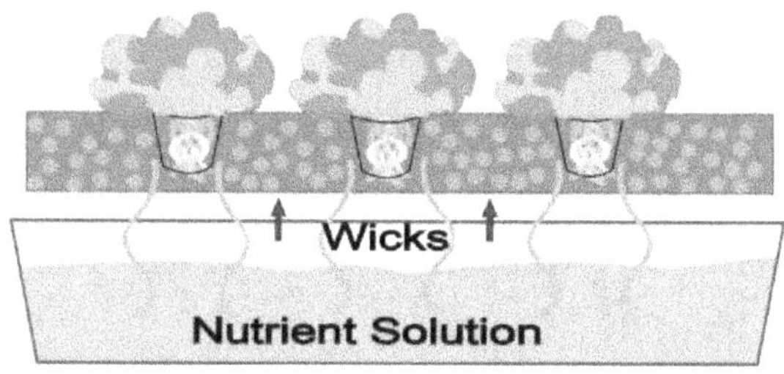

Wick systems are technically the smallest device and the hardest to set up since moving pieces are not necessary. The device comprises a pool loaded with water and nutrients; a tub loaded with a rising medium is above it. Both containers are bound by a wick, which pulls the water loaded with nutrients into the growing medium where it is consumed by plant roots.

This method is perfect for studying the fundamentals, but it does not function well for big plants or water-hungry plants such as salad because the wick can not provide adequate water. Even with microgreens, spices, and peppers, this method fits well.

Water Culture Systems

One easy device to set up is a water history program. In this device, the plants are positioned on the styrofoam framework above the water and nutrient solution tank.

To supply the plant roots with oxygen, a bubbler air pump is connected to the tank. This method is ideal for thirsty plants, though not as appropriate for longer-lasting plants, such as tomatoes.

Ebb and Flow Systems

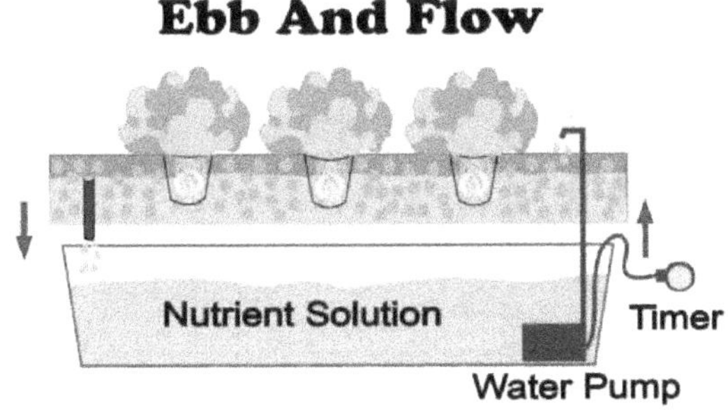

Ebb and flow processes in architecture are much more difficult but still flexible. The method operates by pouring a water nutrient solution into the rising medium and then dumping it back into the reservoir.

To achieve so, the device needs a timer-supported generator. One of the key benefits of ebb and flow is that it helps you to tailor the watering schedule of your plants according to the scale, quantity, atmospheric temperature, moisture, etc. You do have the option of personally customizing potting plants or filling the whole tile with rising medium and planting directly into the tile.

Choosing What to Grow

Almost every plant can be grown hydroponically, but it is a good choice for beginners to start tiny. Herbs and vegetables that grow quickly need limited care and do not need a broad variety of nutrients. Rapidly growing plants are great as they make it easy to evaluate the efficiency and adjustment of the process. It might be a huge letdown to wait for months just to find out that the program doesn't function correctly. Maintenance-free plants are perfect for beginners because they let you focus on thinking about your method—you will then switch to more complicated vegetables. When you develop a number of plants, it is often necessary to ensure that the nutrient needs are identical, such that they develop well together.

Lighting

Hydroponic systems are mostly indoor systems installed where natural sunshine is not available all day long. Most edible plants need a minimum of six hours per day of sunlight, even better 12 to 16 hours. If you do not have a sunroom or another room with a lot of access to the sunlight, you will need additional light to expand.

Hydroponic system kits typically have the requisite light bulbs, but when your own parts are pieced together, you may have to buy different lighting systems.

HID (High-intensity Dish) light fixtures are the perfect illumination for a hydroponic device and may be either HPS (High-Pressure Sodium) or MH (Metal Halide) lamps. The light from HPS bulbs emits a more orange-rot glow, perfect for plants in the stage of vegetative development.

T5 is another kind of illumination used in hydroponic rooms for cultivation. It provides a high performance, low heat, and good energy efficiency fluorescent light. In addition, it is suitable for growing seedlings and plants with limited periods of development.

Put the lighting device on a timer to activate and remove the lights every day at the same moment.

Room Conditions

Another relevant variable to be considered is the room condition; in fact, it is essential to set up a hydroponic device under the right conditions.

Relative precipitation, temperature, CO2 rates, and air movement are the main factors. The optimal moisture for a hydroponic growing region is 40-60 percent relative moisture. Higher rates of moisture—especially in low air circulation rooms—can trigger powdery mildew and other fungal problems.

Ideal temperatures range from 68 ° C to 70 ° C. Hot temperatures will cause the plants to slow down and contribute to rooting rot if the water temperature gets too high.

Your crop region will also have sufficient carbon dioxide (CO2) availability. The best way to ensure this is by maintaining a continuous airflow in the house. More experienced hydroponic gardeners should attach CO2 rates to the room because the more CO2 accessible, the faster the plants expand.

Water Quality

Two factors can influence the capacity of the water to provide the plants with dissolved nutrients: the water mineral salt levels, as determined by PPM, and the water pH. Solid water with a strong mineral content doesn't consume minerals as quickly as water with lower mineral content, so you may need to filter water when the mineral content is heavy. The ideal pH level for water in hydroponic systems varies from 5.8 to 6.2 (slightly acidic). If the water does not follow this requirement, chemical agents can be used to adjust the pH in a sufficient quantity.

Nutrients

The nutrients (or fertilizers) contained in hydroponic systems are available in liquid and dry form as well as inorganic and synthetic form. Every firm may be dissolved into the water for the hydroponic method to generate a combination of nutrients. The primary products you use will contain iron, manganese, boron, zinc, copper, molybdenum and chlorine, and the key macronutrients–nitrogen, potassium, phosphorus, calcium, and magnesium.

Using fertilizers intended for hydroponic gardening, if you use them in compliance with product guidance, will have reasonable performance.

Consider the usage of regular hydroponic plant fertilizer, since the method is formulated for use in garden soil.

Use hydroponic nutrient items to match your needs. Of starters, some are better promoted of flowering plants, whereas others are more useful for encouraging vegetative development, such as leafy greens.

Additional Equipment

Beyond the standard hydroponic system, beginners will invest in a few other things.

Measures are made possible by the pPM and pH of the water and the temperature and relative humidity of the room. Combination meters are used for pH, PPM, and water temperature measurement. You may also buy meters in your rising room to monitor temperature and humidity.

You may need a humidifier or dehumidifier to change relative humidity to an optimum amount in the rising space, depending on your environment.

Yet, you can use any fan or air conditioning equipment in your grow room to boost airflow. Only a basic oscillating fan works great, but you should invest in a more complex intake and exhaust device if you use it more.

Good Starter Plants

Many plants that work really well for beginners to continue to know the fundamentals of hydroponics include:

- Herbs like basil, parsley, oregano, cilantro, and mint
- Greens like lettuce, spinach, Swiss chard, and kale
- Tomatoes
- Hot Peppers
- Strawberries

Systems For More Advanced Gardeners

The NFT method and the aeroponic method are two advanced structures better suited for hydroponic gardeners who have already mastered the fundamentals.

NFT System

NFT stands for Nutrient Film Technique. It requires a water and fertilizer solution that runs continuously into the tray from a tank, where the roots of plants are held in the soil and accumulate nutrients while the fluid passes in. If the pump functions incorrectly, roots will dry easily when the flow ceases, and this device allows a consumer to control the process and repair it rapidly in the case of issues.

Aeroponic System

An aeroponic device is a high-tech method where plant roots are suspended in air and combined with a water and nutrient solution every few minutes. It is a highly effective yet sophisticated pumping and mastering process. If there are issues with the hardware, the roots can dry out and die quickly.

CHAPTER TWO

HYDROPONIC SYSTEMS: WHICH SYSTEM SUITS YOUR NEEDS BY CONSIDERING YOUR BUDGET, TIME, SPACE AND LEVEL OF EXPERIENCE

The way hydroponic systems work could at first seem confusing, but once you understand them, it is actually really simple to see how they function. Hydroponic structures (Drip Method, Ebb & Flow, N.F.T., Water Community, Aeroponics, and Wick) occur in six forms. The roots of plants need three things: water/humidity, nutrients, and oxygen. The six types of hydroponic systems vary clearly by how these three items are transmitted to the plant roots. In the links (by name) to the left and below, each form of device is defined in depth.

Both hydroponic systems, irrespective of what they may name, are focused on those six styles and are either one such system or a mixture of two or more of those six styles. There are thousands of ways to modify and improve every part of each of the six structures. But if you learn all of the three root requirements (water, nutrients, and oxygen) that comes from any form of hydroponic system, you should be able to decide what kind of hydroponic system is easy.

Before Designing and Building a Hydroponic System

Before you build a hydroponic device, it is important to remember the kind of plants that you want to develop there and the room in which they need to develop. You would also continue to build the device to meet plants ' needs (plant scale, root position, root oxygen, water intake, etc.) only after the maximum scale is achieved. While one form of hydroponic system is ideal for growing other types of plants, it might not be the right way to grow certain plants.

The simple points you'd want to note while planning or constructing (even purchases) any hydroponic system are durability and reusability—you would certainly want to use it more than once. You should also worry about how complicated it would be to break it down and extract it to completely clear it during plantings. Often, if you have an issue as plants already grow, think about how challenging it is to repair the issues without destroying the plants or method.

In any sort of hydroponic device, you can develop most plants if you build the system to fit the needs of plants, even when they are complete. It may also be simpler, though, to take less upkeep and to expand it in another form of hydroponic method. Also, it is much easier to cultivate several varieties of plants in various systems meant to be cultivated for these species, rather than attempting to cultivate them all in one big scheme.

Hydroponic System Only Need a Few Basic Parts to Build which includes:

Growing Chamber (or tray)

The growing chamber is the hydroponic environment in which the plants rise. In other terms, the rising chamber is the root zone jar. This field protects plants and also helps the roots to enter the nutrient solution. It also defends the roots from sun, heat, and pesticides. It is essential to keep the root area light and cold. Long lights can hurt roots, and high temperatures in the root area make the plants heat stress and the heat stresses of fruits and flowers.

The size and shape of the increasing chamber depend on the type of hydroponic system the building should create as well as the type of plants. Bigger plants have wider root systems and require more room to hold them in place. The projects are infinite here. You may use almost anything as a rising container; you just don't want some metal because it will corrode and interfere with the nutrients. When you glance around, you can get many suggestions about whether and how you can conveniently use several different items to build your hydroponic system's rising room.

Reservoir

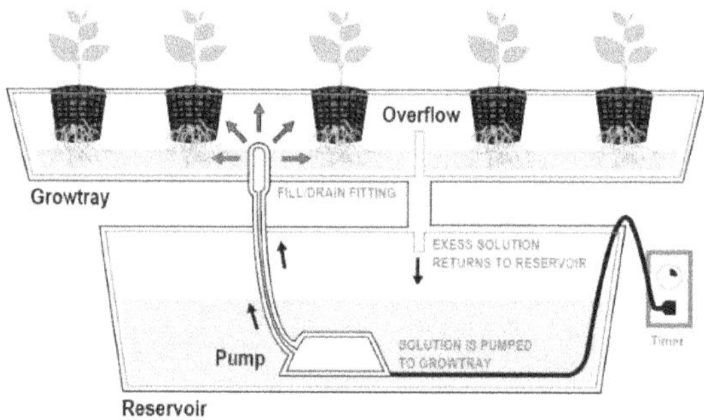

The tank is the hydroponic component of the nutrient solution. The nutrient solution contains crop nutrients combined with water.

The nutrient solution can be circulated from the reservoir to the growing chamber (root zone) in cycles with a timer, or constantly without a timer from the form of hydroponic device, or even the roots may pull down into the reservoir 24/24, rendering the tank the cultivating area.

You may create a pool out of virtually any plastic containing water. Before it spills, it retains ample water, which can be washed first like a tank. A reservoir must also be light-proof. It's not a piece of light evidence, although you can keep it above your head and see the light flowing through it.

Yet every light-proof jar is simple to render by spray, cover, or put anything like a bubble wrap insulation around. Algae and microorganisms can start to develop even with low light.

Submersible Pump

Many hydroponic systems use a semi-submersible pump to pump water from the reservoir to the plant's rising root/chamber region. Throughout the hydroponic hardware store or in most home renovation shops, you can quickly find submerged devices with garden equipment as fountains and pool devices. These are also offered in a wide variety of sizes.

In fact, the submersible pumps are nothing but a spinning impeller which uses an electromagnet. These can even quickly be extracted to be properly washed. When a filter is not used, one may easily be produced by cutting a furnace filter panel or similar material. You will periodically clean the pump and filter to keep it safe.

Delivery system

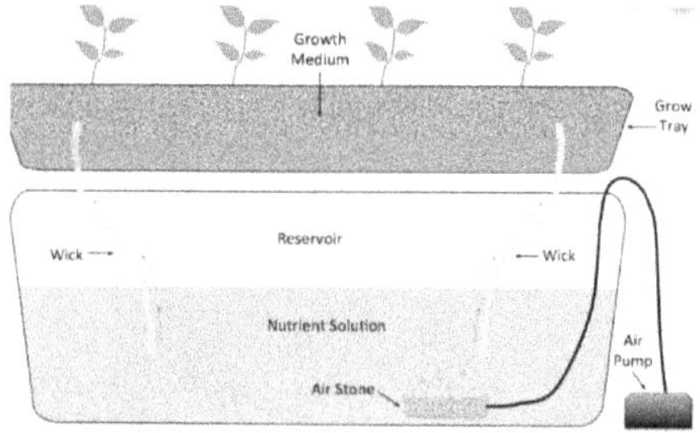

A hydroponic device for water/nutrient solution distribution is very simple and can be highly personalized when constructing your own hydro systems. Measures are made possible by the pPM and pH of the water and the temperature and relative humidity of the room. Usually, a mix of regular PVC tubing and connections, custom tubing for garden irrigation and connections as well as blue or black vinyl tubes is the easiest and safest option for the nutrient supply network.

Depending on the type of hydroponic system you create, drip emitters or sprayers can be needed as part of the distribution mechanism for nutrient solutions. While they can be useful, they can also clog. So, always ensure you have extras you can quickly change with while you clean the clogged ones. A suggestion could be to stop utilizing emitters as they clog and cost extra capital.

Simple Timer

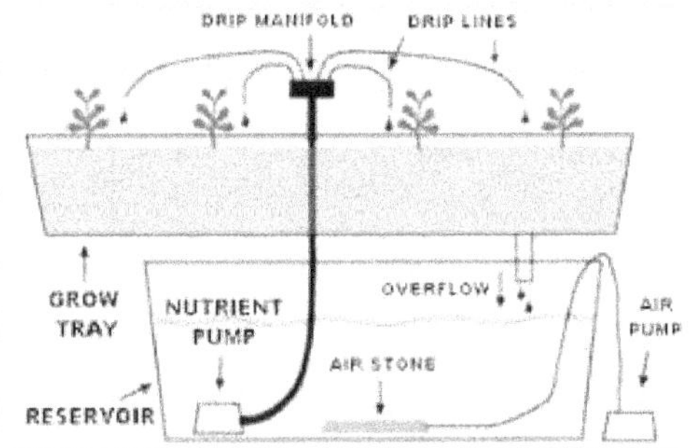

Depending on the sort of hydroponic system you are constructing and the position of your farm, you may need one or two timers. If artificial lighting is being used to develop the plants instead of natural sunlight, you would like the duration of the lighting device to be monitored by a timer. You'll need a timer to monitor the on/off cycles of the submersible water pump for flood and drain, drip, and aeroponic systems. Some forms of aircraft systems may need a special timer.

Default regular light timers operate great on both the lamps and the submersible pumps. The timer should be optimized for fifteen amps rather than ten amps. However, fifteen-amp timers are often considered hard duty if the back of a box or timer is not tested for a level of 15 amp. Opt to buy them for outdoor usage; they typically have a shield and are generally waterproof.

The more costly digital timers are not preferred over the analog dial kind because the digital timers will lose all memory as well as the settings when they lose control or are unplugged for a second (with no battery backup, you can miss it). They also don't have any more actual on/off settings than the analog kind. Only check that the timepiece you get has pins across the button.

Air Pump

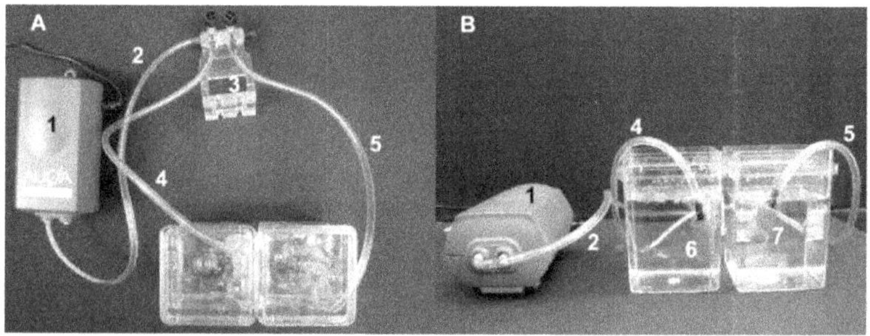

Air pumps are available in hydroponic systems, rather than in water science systems. Yet, their usage has advantages and air pumps are relatively affordable. Anywhere they offer aquarium equipment, air pumps can be purchased. Air pumps mainly provide water and roots with air and oxygen. Air is poured through air stones by an airline to produce a collection of tiny bubbles that grow from the nutrient solution.

In water irrigation systems, the air pump helps protect the plants from suffocating when submerging themselves in the nutrient solution 24/7. The air pump is normally used in the reservoir with some other form of hydroponic device. It helps to increase the volume of dissolved oxygen in the water and to oxygenate the atmosphere.

Another advantage of utilizing air pumps is that when air bubbles rise, water and nutrients pass and disperse, meaning that the nutrients are continuously combined. The flowing oxygenated water often tends to reduce the bacteria in the system.

Grow Lights

Grow lighting is an optional hydroponic device feature. Depending on where you intend to put and develop your hydroponic device, you may either use natural sunlight or artificial light to grow your plants. If you can use it, we choose natural sunlight, it is safe and needs no extra equipment.

However, if there is not adequate natural sunlight to position your hydroponic system, you'll need artificial light to raise your plants.

Grow lights vary from most common household lighting. They are built to emit such colors that mimic natural sunlight. The plants use these light spectrums to conduct photosynthesis (wavelengths). Photosynthesis is needed for plants to cultivate and grow fruit and flowers. The form and light that a plant gets would, therefore, significantly influence the plants ' capacity to photosynthesize and thus grow.

TYPE OF SYSTEMS

1. HYDROPONIC DRIP SYSTEMS

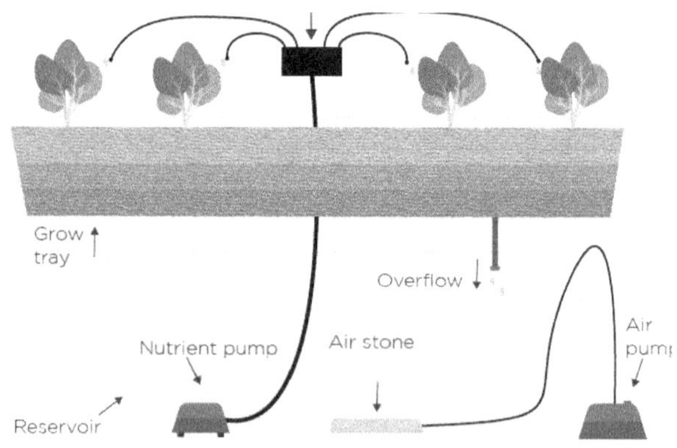

Drip systems are one of the most commonly utilized hydroponic systems in the country for both domestic farmers and company farmers. It is mostly because the principle is simple and needs a few components, but yet it is a rather diversified and efficient hydroponic method. While this is a simple idea, when designing your own structures, it won't hinder your creativity. The way a drip device operates, it allows you to spray nutritional substances on the roots of the plants to hold them moist.

Hydroponic drip systems can be conveniently built from tiny to large systems in several respects. But particularly useful for larger plants with plenty of root room. That is because you don't have to fill the network with vast amounts of water, and the drip lines are quick to extend over larger spaces. Besides using more growing media for larger plants, more growing media retains more moisture than smaller volumes, mainly because it is more forgiving for the plants.

Forgiving that the plants are not as prone to watering hours, and they do not automatically worry whether they are watered on time for one purpose or the other.

What you'll need to build a drip system is:

- A container for the plant's roots to grow in.
- A container (reservoir) to hold the nutrient solution.
- A submersible fountain/pond pump.
- A light timer to turn the pump on and off.
- Several tubing leads from the pump in the tank to the plants (or the drip lines if various types are used).
- Tubing (PVC or flexible tubes) with extra plant nutrient solution for transfer into the tank. (Optional) You can use drip emitters or just place a hot paper clip

in your tubing for a nutrient solution to drip away as you like.

- Growing media for the plants roots to grow in and help support the plants' weight.

The function of a hydroponic drip system is straightforward. Water (nutrient solution) is drained from the tank into tubes up to the seed media (where the plant roots are). From there, it drips through the developing media from the tubing. The nutrient solution removes all the roots and planted media to the bottom of the tub. Thus, the nutrient solution passes into an opening, and gravity allows the solution of nutrients to move downwards through the tank by tubing. It will be recalled that the container plant will be at least 6-8 inches higher than the tip of the tank in order to draw out excess water (water does not surge upward without a pump).

There are really two types of hydroponic drip systems:

a. Recirculating/recovery drip systems

The recirculating drip devices are by far the most widely employed by home growers. The recirculating drip systems sound like they apply to the reuse/cycling of the utilized nutrient solution after it has wet the roots back into the tank, which can be recirculated over and over again via the system. Recirculation systems are often known as recovery systems since the recuperation of the nutrient solution used may be recirculated through the device.

As every hydroponic device recirculating, the nutrient solution in a recycling drip device will alter both pH and nutrient intensity as plants are continuously mixing with nutrients in the water. It ensures that recirculating systems need to test and change pH frequently as required and modify the nutrient solution constantly to maintain a healthy plant nutrient solution.

b. Non-recirculating/non-recovery drip systems

Non-recirculating/non-recovery drip systems are most famous for commercial farmers. Although it looks like a waste of water and nutrients where it can not be retrieved and used again, industrial farmers waste very little. They achieve so by pacing their watering periods accurately. They can change watering times down to the minute, or even second if they need to, using specialized "stage timers."

Also, they just water long enough to moisturize the rising media. Thus water (nutrient solution) is ingested into the plants and held in the growing medium in which plant roots obtain it, and very little of it goes out. They wash the ever-increasing medium with pure freshwater from time to time to prevent build up in the growing medium.

In non-recirculating/non-recovery drips, the nutrient solution appears to have less treatment since, in turn, none of the nutrient solution used is added back to the reservoir. It ensures that you will fill the tank with a healthy, pH-adjusted nutrient solution, and it does not change. As long as the water in the bottle is gradually moving/circulating so that the strong mineral elements do not settle down, a right nutrient solution changed in pH remains.

2. EBB AND FLOW - (FLOOD AND DRAIN) SYSTEM

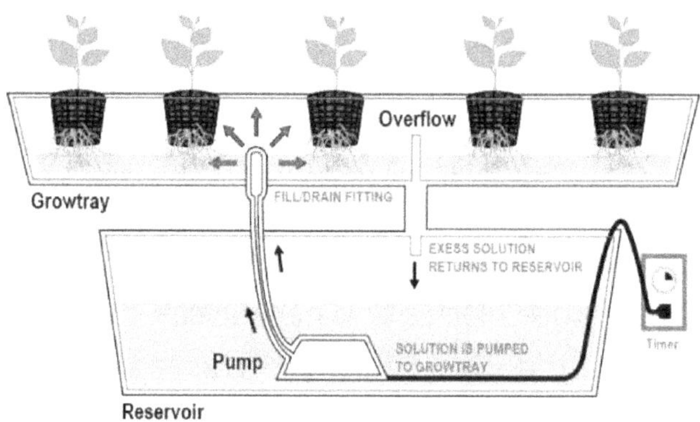

For several purposes, flood and drain systems (ebb and flow) are quite conventional with hydroponic farmers. You can construct them with almost any materials you find around and also expend little money on the hydroponic cultivation of plants. They can also be designed to suit whatever open room you have (either inside or outside), and the different and creative ways to build them for that room are not constrained. Plants thrive very well in flood and drain systems, along with being affordable and straightforward to construct. The flood and drain method operates in theory much as it looks by inserting a nutrient solution into the plant root network - just periodically and not continuously.

How a flood and drain hydroponic system functions very quickly. The central part of the flood and drainage network includes containers in which plants grow. It may be just one plant or several plants in sequence. A timer switches on the valve, and water (nutrient solution) is injected into the main part of the device by tubing from the reservoir using a submersible well/water pump. The nutrient solution fills the network (influxes) until it exceeds the predefined overflow tube height such that the roots of the plants are soaking. The overflow tube would be roughly 2 cm below the top of the rising newspaper.

When the tank is full of water, it flows down through the river, where it is recirculated again into the network. The overflow tube determines the water volume in the flood and drainage network, which guarantees that the water (nutrient solution) will not spill the top of the device as long as the pump is running. When the engine is turned off, the water is pumped back to the river via the pipe.

What you need to create a Flood and Drain network (Ebb and Flow):

- The growing medium of some kind
- A container (reservoir) to hold the nutrient solution.
- A light timer to turn the pump on and off.
- Some tubing to run from thc pump in the reservoir to the system to be flooded.
- A submersible fountain/pond pump.

- An overflow tube set to the height you want the water level.
- A container for the plant's roots to grow in.

There are several different methods of building flood and drainage, and they are perfect for growing small to medium-sized plants. Even for the growth of large plants with more significant flood and irrigation schemes. You can create it with containers, tubing, 2-liter jars, plastic tots, water bottles, an old icebox, garbage cans, etc. You can use just about everything that can hold water. Neither should the creativity end. There are several avenues to overwhelm and empty the foundations of the structure too. Here are several examples of the three most common forms in which the networks become filled and drained.

(Tip 1) Ensure that there is a way through which air will reach through the top without water flowing out. A "T" connection can fit well with an extension a few inches above the waterline. It stops air bubbles arising in the device and guarantees that it leaks and drains correctly.

(Tip 2) Ensure that the overflow channel is wider than the pump water inlet loop. Therefore, since water reaches gravity, and energy falls from the pump by friction, you would inject through more power than the overflow. By doing so, it will allow water to mount up and flow out the top of the tank unless you reduce the pressure (volume) of the pump.

There are basically three main types of flood and drain system setups

a. Plant containers in series design

This form of setup is most prevalent when plant containers are sprayed (flooded) simultaneously.

Please bear in mind that to be adequately watered, the Ebb&Flow flood and irrigation scheme, should be placed above the reservoir – such as on the top of a table or a seat.

Therefore, the water will return to the reservoir with clear gravity and empty the device properly.

The several containers are linked by tubing such that they all overflow equally, at the same moment, as the network becomes overwhelmed. Of ease, there is normally just one overflow tube instead of a different overflow for each pipe being filled. It binds to the base network in which all the containers are linked. So as the water volume hits the height of the runoff, it flows into the Ebb & Flow stream irrigation networks and falls to the river for filtering again into the network. The height of this overflow tube should determine the water level height of all the containers attached to the plants (as long as the water level is).

It is possible to easily change the height of the single overflow tube by adjusting the water height of all of the linked containers.

b. Flooding tray design

The flood table/tree flood and drain (ebb and flow) devices arrangement are helpful if you choose to position structures temporarily in the network, transfer plant around, or put Ebb&Flow flood and drainage table concept plants in another more massive structure. This system floods just one container instead of different containers with plants in it.

A shallow square or rectangular container is normally set on a tray. The reservoir is typically situated immediately below with convenient entry

Ebb&Flow Drain and drain table as flooding water is forced back onto the drain plate on the one side. Then runoff occurs on the other half of the flooded plate. It means that the water properly circulates from one part of the tray to the other. The overflow tube height points out the water height during the flooding process and can be changed if appropriate, equivalent to any flooding and drain device (ebb and flow).

The plants are produced in traditional plastic pots or containers and are placed as typically potted plants in a flood tank. Unlike ordinary potted plants, though, hydroponic seed media are used for potting the plants instead of utilizing potted dirt. Once the plants are big enough, they may be transferred to a permanent hydroponic facility.

The development of algae is one of the downsides of the flood table and should be cleaned up periodically. Since the top of the tray normally stays open, the light may penetrate the nutrient solution at the bottom of the tray, enabling algae to expand. While the algae itself is not harmful to the plants, they require dissolved oxygen in the water.

c. Serge tank flood and drain (ebb and flow) system design

The flood and drainage style serge tank is useful if more vertical space is needed. The reservoir is usually smaller than the Ebb&Flow Flood and Drain Schemes than the serge tank network of flood and drainage systems.

The nutrient solution, so the water in this case, will run back into the tank through the leak. It will happen when the pump is off from the device through the way of gravity.

But even though the amount of water in the reservoir is more considerable than the hydroponic method, it is always possible to set up a flood and drain device - it refers to the usage of a surge tank.

The flood and drainage device style sergeant tank costs more as far more parts are required. It operates on the major Ebb&Flow Flood and drainage networks in an inundation process with a surge tank that is built for its own depth. In other terms, when attached under the waterline, the water height in one container would be the same in another container. The surge tank acts as temporary storage that maintains the height of the water in all the containers with their plants and is only completely loaded during the flooding process.

Ebb&Flow Pump and drain mechanisms in the pumping process serge tank device stream, and drain (ebb and flow) is controlled from the far larger main tank by the pumping water (nutrient solution) to the serge tank while the pump timer is used. If the water volume in the serge tank decreases, the water level in all the related containers of the plant rises equally. A float valve in the Ebb&Flow Flood and drainage networks of serge tanks is turned on in the serge tank. The device in the serge tank then transfers water to the main tank. The two pumps are actually on (pump in the central reservoir and surge tank).

When the pump timer in the main reservoir is turned off, the engine in the serge tank stays running. The pump in the serge tank drains all the water back into the main tank (power drainage) before the water volume is too small. A second float valve shuts off the pump in the sergeant tank at that stage.

3. N.F.T. (NUTRIENT FILM TECHNIQUE) SYSTEM

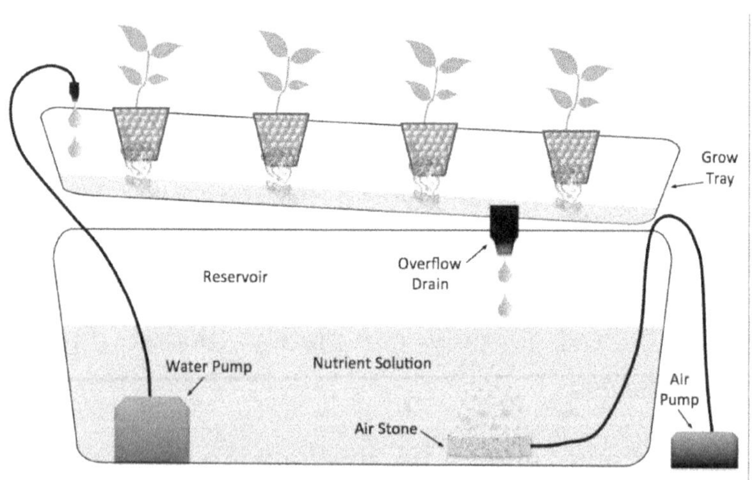

The N.F.T. (Nutrient Film Technique) method is also prevalent with domestic hydroponic farmers because of its straightforward design.

The N.F.T. schemes, though, are better suited to grow smaller plants such as different varieties of lettuce, which are more widely utilized.

In addition to increasing kale, several industrial farmers often develop various kinds of herbs and baby greens utilizing N.F.T. systems.

Although an N.F.T. method is built in a variety of different forms, they have the same function as a very shallow nutrient hydroponic solution.

Where the bare roots of the plants touch the water and may consume the nutrients, the biggest drawback to an N.F.T. device is that the plants are particularly vulnerable to water movement interruptions from power outages (or some reason).

Once the water starts flowing into the network, the plants can continue to wind very rapidly.

What you need to build an N.F.T. system:

- Container to hold the nutrient solution (a reservoir)
- Submersible fountain/pond pump
- Tubing to distribute water from the pump to the N.F.T. growing tubes
- Growing tubes for the plants to grow in (also called a gully/channel)

- starter cubes, or small baskets and growing media to start seedlings in.
- Return system (tubing, channels) to guide the used nutrient solution back to the reservoir

The structure and the functioning of a hydroponic N.F.T. system is generally not complicated. The nutrient solution from the tank is transferred to a converter that links a variety of smaller tubes with the larger channel. Each of these smaller tubes is supplied with the plants from one side of one of the growing channels.

The nutrient solution is made up of a thin layer (film) that flows through each channel with the plants on the other side, passing through each plant and wetting roots down the channel.

Yet, the nutrient solution passes from one hand to the other as the canal is strongly angled such that the stream moves down the slope.

Usually, seedlings in the growing tubes with rising media in small holes on the top of the tube are held above the surface. The seedlings' roots are hanged out to the bottom of the tube, which offers nutrients from the low film of the nutrient solution.

The excess resource solution flows out of the bottom end of a pipe falls into another canal or conduit and recirculates back to the reservoir.

Although the nutrient solution flowing through the channels is very shallow, the entire plant root mass stays moist from the roots and is capable of moisturizing outside the roots as well as humidity within the tube.

The roots floating between the plant base and the water level in the pipe not only provide exposure to nutrients, but they may also be supplied with a lot of oxygen from the air above them in the tube.

Commercial farmers typically use specially designed N.F.T. systems that have smooth surfaces with grooves that extend longitudinally along the pipe. Such grooves enable water to pass through the root mass, which keeps it from being dammed.

Home farmers also use vinyl rain gutters for their pipes. These spouts have identical grooves, but cost just a fraction of the cost of commonly made channels.

Yet, home farmers also use N.F.T. Circular tubing ADS (Advanced Irrigation System) programs. There are no grooves in the ADS tubing, but the oval tube still better matches the pitch to compensate.

N.F.T. system Flow rate, and channel slope

The two most commonly posed questions regarding this sort of structure are how deep the water will be and how quickly it will run. The canal slope first regulates the speed at which the water flows into the pipe (not the water pump or).

Usually, the suggested pitch for an N.F.T. device is 1:30 to 1:40. This means a one-inch drop (slope) is suggested for every 30 to 40 inches of horizontal range.

Also, it is suggested to realize the N.F.T. system in a way that it is possible to change the direction while plans also grow eventually.

That is because as the root systems become bigger, they can allow the water flow to pool and dam up. You can turn it further if you like to change because it is customizable. Seek to make the channels as real as possible while designing the N.F.T. programs. Water will accumulate in certain places as it falls into holes.

The required N.F.T. device flow rate usually varies from 1/4 to 1/2 gallon per minute per tube (1 to 2 liters) per tube. Or 15 to 30 gallons an hour (60 to 120 liters). Although the plants are just seeds, the required flow rate should be halved and then increasing as the seeds expand. Flow concentrations are far higher or lower than those often related to nutrient deficiencies. Nutrient deficiencies were often noticed as the channels (gully) expand over 30 to 40 feet (10 to 15 meters) were often observed. However, a second nutrient feeder line halfway across the tube (channel) has been seen to eliminate this issue.

4. WATER CULTURE SYSTEM

Water systems are the easiest of the six hydroponic systems types. Technically, these systems are still very successful in hydroponic cultivation. Not only do home hydroponic farmers prefer to use water culture systems, but industrial producers also do utilize this form of the device on a broad scale.

The reason is that water cultivation systems are a clear and easy idea to develop. Moreover, the fact that the water system is also a cheap device to create is another explanation of why it is also popular with home growers.

While the principle is necessary, there are lots of creative ways of utilizing and constructing water culture systems from different materials.

What you need to build a Water Culture system:

- Aquarium air pump
- Container to hold the nutrient solution (reservoir)
- Airline/hose
- Baskets, pots, or cups to hold the plants
- Air stones (or soaker hose) to create the small bubbles
- Some type of growing media

A hydroponic water culture system is simple to use. The plant is held just above the nutrient solution in bins in the reservoir. Hydroponic Water Culture System on top or via troughs created in the reservoir cover. The roots remain out of the baskets in which the plants are mounted and collapse into the nutrient solution directly; the origins are continuously submerged 24 hours a day.

The roots are not suffocating since air and oxygen are formed by air bubbles, which are created by a combination of nutrients and dissolved oxygen in the water.

The more air bubbles, the better for water culture systems. The bubbles will make the water appear like boiling water at a fast rolling boil. The bubbles should be raised in direct touch with the roots as they rise to the top of the water such that the plants can be most efficient. There are currently two methods to supply the nutrient solution with aeration and dissolved oxygen.

TYPES OF AERATION

a. Air bubbles

Aquarium air pumps and air stones usually have the fertilizer solution for water irrigation systems and certain forms of hydroponic systems of air bubbles. The air pump supplies air pressure and has an airline attached to air stones. The air stones are made of a porous rock-like material; the small pores produce tiny single bubbles of air that rises to the top of the surface.

Short of air bricks, soaker tubes may also be used to produce air bubbles. The soaker tube produces only smaller bursts of dust. The lower the air bubbles, the further the mineral solutions will be aerated. Smaller air bubbles provide the water with additional touch area. The interaction between the air and water bubbles helps remove the depleted oxygen from the roots of the plants.

b. Falling water

Whereas this surface disruption is not usual to household farmers in water cultivation systems, falling water is just another effective way to aerate the nutrient solution. The more the temperature drops, the smaller the impact until it meets the surface of the ocean. The lower the power, the higher the chaos and more aeration are given (dissolved oxygen). This aeration approach is more prevalent in commercial water cultivation systems because large amounts of water are used relative to domestic cultivators.

c. Recirculating Water Culture systems

The recirculating water culture method is another variant of the traditional water culture framework. The recirculation device acts as a flood and irrigation network, but it never drains. You may have as many rising containers (water culture storage tanks) as you like in a central storage tank.

Each container in cultivation has its own filling line and an overflow channel that drains back into the main container.

Some farmers are using buckets rather than massive, shallow containers. Each bucket has its own plant and is packed with a rough solution of nutrients - you may have a series of such containers.

By using a fountain or a pond pump, each bucket pumps the nutrient solution. While the water fills the containers, the excess water leaks into the overflow channel, and, in the meantime, it flows back to the tanks where the fluid is recirculated.

Most growers who recirculate the nutrient solution for their water cultivation systems only use an air pump in the central reservoir, instead of in each specific bucket (especially to save money). They require the water pump to operate 24 hours a day. But if you have air bubbles flowing like a traditional water crop device in each tank, you will change the period of the water pump. Furthermore, plants benefit from close interaction with growing air bubbles that touch the roots.

The recirculation of the water helps you to use dropping water as an aeration source in the device. You do not also need to have to test water levels in each tub to refill the water that the plants drained (you only examine and recycle them in the central reservoir). About all large commercially-run water irrigation systems recirculate water across the system.

DWC (Deep Water Culture)

The word "DWC" is frequently misused when water systems are represented. So why is "DWC" not one of six forms of hydroponic systems? What is "DWC?" Well, to start with, the DWC system isn't a special kind of hydroponic device.

As the full name of' Deep Water Culture indicates, this is only a modification of the current form of hydroponic system recognized as a water culture method. The term "huge" is only used to define other water culture structures if the network water depth is 8-10 inches lower than that of the existing DWC system.

However, irrespective of water depth, DWC systems continue to be water cultivation systems.

Much of the time, the diameter of the water/nutrient solution will not be smaller than 8 inches. It is only applicable for bigger plants with broader root systems, which need far more room and much more water. Or when using a container such as a bucket that must be loaded large enough to properly reach the main root ball of plants near the top. Plants such as the scale of most lettuce varieties can be grown with only 4-6 inches of water in water culture systems.

Today, there is no distinction between how a traditional water culture system works or works with a DWC (deep water cultivation). It is exactly the same, the only difference is the system's water density.

Whether a traditional water cultivation method, a real DWC system, or even a circular standard water culture system or an actual DWC system, you still want to ensure that the plants are provided with sufficient water volume and proper oxygenation of the root system. Even if they get full scale.

The volume of water is separate from the height of water. When you take a gallon of water and dump it into a large container, the height of the water can only be one inch or two across, but placing the same water gallon into a 3-inch deep bowl, the height of the water would be nearer to 2 feet. And the quantity and height of water are two completely separate things. There's more on how much water volume you can use per vine in this eBook!

Should the water level be above or below the baskets?

There is always ambiguity and maybe even debate on where the amount of water/nutrient solution will be in water cultivation systems. Should the basket reach or hang over the water? There are both positives and drawbacks, so there's no right or wrong. The water level in a water culture environment may also be rapidly and efficiently adjusted by merely introducing more water or withdrawing it.

When the air bubbles reach the top of the water, they are already on the surface of the water. As they fall, they scatter small water droplets one to two inches off the surface of the atmosphere. The degree to which such tiny water outlets are dispersed primarily depends on how much air is currently supplied and how much air bubbles are sprayed from the air stones to the soil.

If the container does not touch the water and sits only above it, these little droplets of sprinkling water hold the rising media moist near to the bottom of the baskets. How wet depends on how often air bubbles emerge and scatter on the surface of the water around the container.

A strong analogy is that it is related to boiling water (massive rolling boil, rolling boil, heating, just cooking). With a heavy rolling boil being best and only a minimal cooling. Another factor is the sort of rising media used is another aspect. Many growing media can retain and keep moisture faster and smoother than some, which often creates a huge difference.

If the basket touches the surface, the growing media in the baskets can absorb more surface than if they hang over it, so this can be helpful.

Yet, the form of media in which they expand again can make a big difference as certain growing media consume and retain moisture quicker and better than others. Therefore, water may be logged at the bottom of the baskets absolutely because it is in continuous touch with the surface.

If so, either lower the water level such that the baskets hang above the surface, or use a specific form of medium.

It is also necessary to note that the size of the plant often varies. The roots of the plants would collapse in the application of water and nutrients. In other terms, roots can go and grow anywhere they have moisture.

When the plant is tiny, and the roots have not yet developed out of the bottom of the container, it may be useful for the baskets to enter the water. At least before the roots expand back and stay underwater long enough

even as the bottom of the baskets are lovely and damp with the tiny droplets of water sprinkling and air bubbles floating above it. The extra humidity next to the plant root ball from the rising media that directly stirs water/nutrient solution when the baskets contact the water will stimulate root growth, while plants and root mass are low.

The Kratky Method

First of all, I would clarify that the process named Kratky is not a modern or unique form of hydroponic device. It's only a modification of a typical water culture scheme, but then it was usually called by the name of a human (renamed). To my understanding, the adjustment has been called the Kratky

Process after B.A. Kratky at the University of Hawaii, who teaches hydroponic techniques without recirculation.

Hydroponic systems that are not recirculated (also known as "run to waste systems") do not pump water/nutrient solution from the tank through the plants or back to the tank.

In fact, they also inject water from the tank to the plants and either dump the water/nutrient solution into the field or into a drainage network to remove the leakage.

It seems inefficient, but non-recirculating systems can be advantageous and can run low if performed correctly. By nature, water culture systems are not recirculating, but may also be changed as circulation systems.

The hydroponic method, often referred to as the Kratky cycle, is essentially an air pump-free water culture device and component NFT method.

It is a method of water culture as plants hang over the water/nutrient pool in which the roots live.

Also, it is a part of the NFT method because there is a difference between the basket containing the plant and the water containing the roots in the NFT schemes. This void reflects an air pocket that must replace the air pump in a standard water network.

The basket will reach the water when the plants are low so that the roots may rise from the base. When plants expand, and the roots get more significant, the plant often absorbs some water.

It lowers the water depth, which creates an air void. Since the air pump removes the dissolved oxygen and oxygenates the water, the air difference is required for the plant to receive the oxygen. This type of system design is useful where there is no or unreliable electricity.

Nonetheless, these approaches have definite drawbacks. The air pump supplies more than dissolved oxygen in water cultivation systems. The rising bubbles keep the water moving. The mineral salts (nutrients) settle down next to the floor while the solution of water/nutrients becomes inert.

It contributes to inconsistent nutrient distribution (extremely high near to the bottom and very low close to the top). The growing air bubbles from the air pump create movement in the water, which maintains the nutrient solution constantly mixing and, thus, also spread nutrients equally over the surface.

Furthermore, although the roots of plants are able to obtain oxygen through the Kratky process, nutrients come from the roots above the waterline, and the roots below the water line can not receive oxygen because they have already dissolved oxygen in the soil at an early stage and nothing can substitute it. For the plant, this is a cause of tension. Think of it as if you're in the swimming pool without being able to shift because you have the nose above the water so that you can breathe, and keeping your mouth below the surface to drink water so that you don't dehydrate. If you had to endure, it would be very painful.

Plants are adaptable and often seek to change the best they can to their climate and setting. However, the conditions given by the Kratky system are far from ideal. The cost of running an air pump 24/7 and replacing dissolved oxygen is meager while they are far less ideal conditions. The Kratky approach may be a valuable and effective alternative in places where power is extremely unstable or non-existent.

5. AEROPONIC SYSTEM

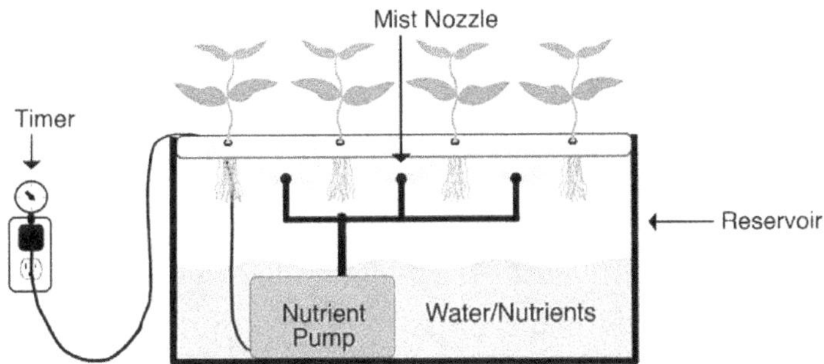

Although the aeroponic system is a fundamental term, it is, in reality, the most advanced of all six types of hydroponic systems. Nonetheless, constructing your own aeroponic system is very simple, and several home growers love to grow in them and even get outstanding results with this kind of hydroponic device.

As in every other form of hydroponic device, you may use a variety of different styles of materials and design configurations to suit your room - It can be applied even if your room and your creativity are tiny.

Aeroponic structures usually use little or no rising media with certain advantages. The roots produce full oxygen, and as a result, the plants expand faster.

Yet, aeroponic systems do typically require less water than some other form of hydroponic device. Harvesting, particularly for root crops, is typically also easier.

However, there are still certain drawbacks of aeroponic devices in addition to being more costly to construct. The sprinkler heads will obstruct the creation of the dissolved mineral elements in the watertight of nutrients. Be sure you have extras to swap with when they clog while you clean them.

Moreover, since the plant roots remain in the center of the air through nature in aeroponic systems, the roots of plants are far more prone to dry up if the irrigation process is disrupted. Only a temporary power loss (for whatever reason) would, therefore, cause your plants to die far faster than any other form of hydroponic system. There is also a reduced margin of error with nutrient rates, particularly true high-pressure systems in aeroponic systems.

What you'll need to build your own basic Aeroponic system:

- The water source tubing from the reservoir pumps to the heads of the mister in the through the room.
- Container to hold the nutrient solution (a reservoir).

- Submersible fountain/pond pump.
- Tubing to return the excess nutrient solution back to the reservoir.
- Enclosed growing chamber for the root zone.
- Mister/sprinkler heads.
- Watertight container for the growing chamber where the plants' root systems will be.
- Timer (preferably a cycle timer) to turn on and off the pump.

The function of the aeroponic device is a relatively basic term. First of all, the roots aim is to get as much oxygen as possible in mid-air. The high oxygen the roots get allows the plants to grow faster than otherwise and the key benefit of that form of hydroponic system.

Second, if some growing medium is used, revealing all plant roots, there is usually very little. Whether tiny buckets or closed-cell foam plugs that trap the plants are suspended, these baskets or foam plugs fit in the top of the growing chamber.

The roots hang inside the rising container, where they are sprayed on regular short cycles with the nutrient solution by the master heads. The daily irrigation cycles keep the roots moist and dry and provide the nutrients required for the plants to grow.

The growing chamber in which pressure is located should be light and airtight. There must be new air around the roots so that they can get lots of nutrients, but on the other hand, the risk could derive from potential bacteria or plagues to come around.

You ought to hold the root chamber in moisture so that it gets a lot of water, new air, and nutrients. A well-designed aeroponic system provides the three combos high-pressure gently with a good balance to the heart.

Finally, the water droplet scale is a significant element in aeroponic systems. Roots sprinkled with fine nebula can expand even quicker, bushier, and with more places to draw nutrients and oxygen with small streams of water, including tiny sprinkler heads.

It frequently ensures that the plant canopy rose fountain cell forms are defined by the scale of the water droplet.

CHAPTER THREE

WHAT IS THE BEST GROWING MEDIUM FOR HYDROPONICS?

You typically see plants developing in nutrient-rich soil when dreaming of plant production. Yet you don't need dirt for hydroponics. The plants are instead slow-quality, a mineral nutrient solution based on water. They do require a growing medium in which to develop, often known as the substratum.

The best growth rising climate fully system depends on the option of method.

The most common choices of growing media are;

Grains and Pebbles

- Lightweight expanded clay aggregate
- Perlite
- Vermiculite

Foam Matrix

- Rockwool
- Oasis cubes

Fibrous Organic Material

- Coco coir
- Parboiled rice husks
- Pine bark

What Role Does The Growing Medium Play In Hydroponics?

In addition to supporting the weight of the plant, it serves to provide the root system with moisture and oxygen and access to the nutrients it needs.

What Are The Advantages to Using A Growing Medium Other Than Soil?

One of the key benefits is that it prevents the risk of crop pests and diseases. It also ensures that you will produce goods in fields with low-quality conditions–even where there is no such thing as patios, roofs, or even internal regions.

And no crops, no plants! It also helps you to monitor the rising climate adequately, from the temperature to the amount of humidity and oxygen to the nutrients. Best of all, if their roots do not need to check desperately for the nutrients they need in soil, the plants can grow quicker and healthier.

The Importance of Choosing The Right Growing Medium for Hydroponics

Most media styles may be used for growing plants. For example, you probably already know the peat moss.

Inorganic substances such as sand, gravel, and growstone made of recycled glass and organic products, such as pine bark and coconut the growing also soil, are used in growing media in hydroponics.

If you select which tool you will use for your hydroponic project, considerations including the plants that you expect to develop to the prices and quality of the different media need to be taken into account. The critical element, though, is the form and configuration of the device you plan to create.

While all the hydroponic systems and devices that you are willing to use are somewhat different, the aim is still the same: you want moisture from plant roots but not too much. When the medium is continuously filled with water, the roots will suffocate due to lack of oxygen, which results in a root rot that destroys the plant.

What Are The Main Forms of Growing Media Used in Hydroponics?

Hydroponics may be divided into three primary forms: grain and pebbling, foam matrix, and organic fibrous matter. The growing method may be used for individual or general purposes and is especially appropriate for a particular type of hydroponic cultivation system.

Grains and Pebbles

This sort of growth medium helps plants, along with aeration and room to rise and extend plant roots. Most often provide heat, although some provide drainage.

This eBook discusses the use of the following grain-type media:

- Lightweight expanded clay aggregate
- Growstones
- Perlite

- Vermiculite
- Superabsorbent polymer
- River rock
- Sand

In addition, despite recommendations for related products, you may even use lightweight pumice stone or gravel.

Foam Matrix

Foam matrix media that make excellent hydroponic substrate include:

- Rockwool
- Oasis cubes
- Floral foam
- Open-cell flexible polyurethane foam

Fibrous Organic Matter

Fibrous organic matter has a composition of grains and matrices that comprises of individual particles, but they shape a fibrous bulk.

Here are the main forms of organic fibrous products used for hydroponic growth mentioned in the last portion of this article:

- Coco coir
- Parboiled rice husks
- Pine bark
- Pine shavings

Sheep wool is not yet commonly used, but it is growing popularity as a promising organic, sustainable fibrous hydroponic process.

Hydroponic System Growing Media Needs

Let us take a look at the different hydroponic systems and what types of growing media are required until we come to the list of growing media used for hydroponics.

Water Culture Systems

In water systems, plants are suspended through a reservoir, so their roots spread directly into nutritionally rich oxygenated water.

You're going to use a medium that gives some stability but does not add too much humidity to your starters or tiny rising containers, so only the bottom is moisturized while the top stays dry. If the medium becomes too warm, it may make stem purple.

Rising rock and Rockwool are two media widely used in systems for water processing.

Nutrient Film Technique Systems

The most common continuous-flow solution culture, Nutrient Film Technique (NFT), is another method that requires only increasing media to start your plants since the roots grow directly in the washing solution. As is the case for water propagation plants, only the bottom of the starting cube or basket medium will be moist in order to prevent stem purple.

Aeroponic Systems

In comparison, aeroponic systems need only a growing medium of seed, cuttings, and transplants. Again, by using a medium that does not consume too much water while feeding nutrients into the roots of plants, it is necessary to prevent stalking red.

Wick Systems

With no engines, pumps, or moving parts to provide the plant roots with a nutrient solution, a growing medium is necessary to absorb and retain moisture in wick systems. Lightweight, absorbent fabrics such as perlite and cocoa are among these systems most appropriate mediums.

Flood and Drain Systems

For flood and drainage schemes, flood media such as perlite and vermiculite should be prevented because the flowing water literally washes it down. Effective drainage is what you need for these devices. When you grow trellis plants such as peas, tomatoes, or melons, you will use a habitat that will stay dry during floods and retain support for your crops.

For such processes, rising stones are a good alternative, because they have drainage and do not retain too much humidity. Another right choice would be to put down river stones under another medium, such as coconut chips, that carry sufficient moisture to supply the roots with nutrients during the drainage stage.

Drip Systems

With a proper drainage, the moisture in drip systems can be easily managed. You should place a medium-sized like river stones down here again and use a material like pine shavings that will bind the plants to moisture.

HYDROPONIC GROWING MEDIA: THE ULTIMATE LIST

And now it is here: a detailed (but not exhaustive) list of hydroponic media.

Lightweight Expanded Clay Aggregate

A pervasive medium for hydroponics is Lightweight Expanded Clay Aggregate (LECA). LECA substrate is often classified as rock developing, clay pellets and clay pellets, as well as different products, through firing round pellets of clay, in a manner that allows the clay to spread like popcorn such that it is brittle, lightweight yet strong enough to offer your plants decent help.

It is a clean, pH-neutral medium and, overtime doesn't compact. It can be used again, even though it should be washed and re-sterilized on a full scale. LECA is readily accessible from manufacturers of hydroponics.

Growstones

Growstones are made of recycled material, they are a little like LECA. Also, they are durable, elastic, and lightweight.

Growstones include maximum humidity and percenters the potential to wave water up to four inches above the waterline of your hydroponic device.

It indicates that you will be cautious not to leave the upper part of your rising medium wet, contributing to stem purple. This dilemma can be solved by providing proper ventilation or provide exchangeability that is adequately deep enough in case rainfall doesn't reach up.

Perlite

Perlite is a superheated mineral that becomes very lightweight, pH-neutral, elastic, and incredibly absorbent pebbles. It is also paired with other that media to reduce the accumulation of water.

Perlite may also be used by itself, but it is not suitable for flood and irrigation systems construction since it is so light that it floats. You will be vigilant when dealing with perlite so as not to get any of the dust in your eyes. Before working with it, spray it down to clean it and remove airborne debris.

Throughout gardening centers, you might quickly find bagged perlite because it is sometimes blended into potting soils. But if you want to save some energy, look at building suppliers that offer it as a cement additive.

Vermiculite

Vermiculite is another silicate mineral somewhat close to perlite but has a greater exchangeability to store unused minerals as required later on.

Vermiculite is often used for other applications, including perlite. However, only vermiculite for horticultural use can be purchased.

Superabsorbent Polymer

A super absorbent polymer (SAP), often known as water crystal gel, water beads, and slush powder, can produce large liquid volumes due to its weight. SAP has numerous applications, from aqueous solutions for diapers, adult incontinence products, feminine hygiene products, and large-scale flood management schemes, as well as their use in potting and other soils for the storage of moisture.

The beads are inexpensive and durable and are distributed in many sizes, with bigger sizes being better used as a hydroponic method of processing. As previously described, larger granules require more air space within the substratum, needed for ventilation and root development. It is especially relevant for water beads as they expand and become a gel-like material. These should be combined with a particular granular solution to maximize the flow of oxygen to the plant roots.

River Rock

While water can not be absorbed by river rock, it can also be used as a hydroponic medium to expand. The irregular shapes allow the plant roots to expand and provide a lot of oxygen in the gaps between the rocks. You also need to ensure the water is provided often enough so the roots don't get too dry. Or you can blend with another tool that allows water to supply the plants with sufficient moisture.

River rock is probably only used in conjunction with other mediums to help remove water. It is sometimes positioned at the bottom of the container, of which the primary substrate is saturated.

Also, river rock may usually be bought in several different sizes at home improvement shops and Aquafina-grained shops. You may use some typical stones, even though they don't have the smooth and rounded edges of real rocky rivers to produce the same effects. But you must first clean and sanitize before you use them by sprinkling the soil, rubbing it with cloth, and rinsing it

Sand

Sand is another growing medium that can be inexpensive and readily accessible, just very heavy. Just like river blocks, sand is also combined with other products such as perlite, vermiculite, and chocolate, which tend to maintain and aerate humidity. It all adds to the weight issue.

If you are trying to use sand as a growing hydroponic medium, Rockwool large grains rather than the exquisite, fine-grained sand contained in the most glamorous beaches of the world, the bigger size provides more air pockets between the grains.

You need to clean it before use to get as much of the dust particles out of it as you can- it always has to be sterilized before an operation.

Rockwool

Rockwool is a material most commonly used in hydroponics, which is usually made of granite or limestone and is warmed up to a molten state and then spun at high speed, resulting in an interwoven matrix of delicate fibers. Hydroponics is outstanding as it is clean, not degradable, and brittle can retain loads of water and air and has a strong foundation that ensures plants are secure, making it a common alternative for starter cubes.

Rockwool has to be trained until it is used to develop plants to maintain the correct pH balance.

Oasis Cubes

Oasis cubes are identical to Rockwool but allow density to get trapped in mud, as long as they are not in direct contact with water. Oasis cubes, like Rockwool, is mostly used as starter blocks, but can also be used to build the entire hydroponic system.

Oasis cubes mimic the foam used in floral white to hold the stems in their flower displays. They absorb air and water, walk humidity through the medium, and enable plant roots to expand through the open-cell structure of the soil.

Floral Foam

Floral foam can also be used as a growing medium in hydroponics because it absorbs water well.

However, you have to ensure that the vapor is not in continuous touch as it can easily be absorbed by the salt. However, be mindful that it appears to collapse and that the water source becomes vulnerable to stray debris.

Open-Cell Flexible Polyurethane Foam

The low-density foam used for bedding and insulation is classified as open-cell polyurethane foam (FPF), which is another matrix-type substratum substitute. Big in clothing and hobby markets, FPF comes in rolls in various sizes and thicknesses that can conveniently be sliced into a bigger tub or starter cubes.

On the hydroponics stage, FPF is relatively recent. And while it isn't necessarily some moist/hydroponic manufacturers bring, innovators use it to find an inexpensive solution to unique matrix substrates such as Rockwool and oasis cubes.

Coco Coir

Coir is a fibrous fiber from the coconut husk. Though synthetic, coir gradually decomposes such that no mineral is released to growing plants. It is good hydroponics growing medium because its pH is neutral, and it retains moisture well and provides excellent aeration for plant roots.

For hydroponics, coir is used in two separate forms: coconut fiber, close to potting compost, and coconut chips, which are much like tiny woodchips. Coco chips are the perfect option for plant baskets and cases in which you need to ensure the roots receive enough oxygen.

Both types of cocoa are available in compressed bricks, which expand in water by about five-six times the size. If you soak your coir many times using moist/hot water, it won't tint the water source in your hydroponic method.

Parboiled Rice Husks

Like chocolate, parboiled rice husks (PRH) are an organic commodity that can be used as a hydroponic medium, because they break down very gradually. After milled rice, the husks are steamed and dried for the destruction of pathogens such as fungi, fungal spores, and rotting bugs.

PRH has a pH spectrum that is ideal for most plants grown hydroponically and it is also combined with another form like pine bark.

Rice husks can be used in many ways like fresh and composted husks, but usually, because of the high likelihood of pollutants, such types are not included in hydroponics. Their strong manganese centers are another issue. However, manganese toxicity will not be a concern if the substance has a pH above five, which for hydroponics is below average.

Pine Bark

One of the first substrates known to be used in hydroponics was pine bark. Pine is a favored tree bark since it is easier to decompose and contains less toxic acids than other barks that may be leached.

Three forms of pine bark exist: young, composted and aged. You need to apply extra nitrogen to your nutrient solution if you use fresh pine bark because fresh pine bark requires nitrogen before it starts to break down. The use of composted pine bark will prevent this issue. Older pine bark contains more nitrogen than young ones.

When a waste product is deemed useless, pine bark is commonly used as a mulch and an appealing floor cover and even for hydroponics. In planting and landscaping centers, you can conveniently locate it.

Pine Shavings

Pine shavings are another affordable and widely accessible option in pet and feed shops. It is used for hamster and bunny cages and horse stalls. You just have to be alert to scan every packet to verify that there are no artificial odor inhibitors or fungicides. It can also be produced from oven-dried wood, which indicates the toxic sap has been burnt.

Do not be inclined to consider using sawdust as a hydroponic tool, because it is compacted if hot. Even if you use the largest pine shavings around, you need to be vigilant because the substratum gets trapped. The river rock should also be put at the bottom of the container to ensure proper drainage.

CHAPTER FOUR

UNDERSTAND THE ROLE OF NUTRIENTS AND LIGHTING FOR HEALTHY, PROSPEROUS GARDENS

NUTRIENTS

Nutrients shape the backbone of every hydroponic device, so it is essential to know what you are providing and what could go wrong as we will fulfill all the plant nutritional specifications. For every nutrient solution, the quality of the nutrient is the two variables to be addressed first–whether it includes all the elements required for the plant growth in the right ratios. Secondly, your healthy and full nutrient solution will give you the intensity or 'EC' for your particular crop, growth stage, and form of hydroponic device.

The nutrient solution – composition

Many farmers prefer a 'pre-mixed' nutrient solution that merely needs to be condensed (for liquid concentrates) or dissolved before usage in water. These pre-made nutrients are also provided in 2, 3, 4, or more sections so that a grower may adjust the ratio of the minerals to enable either fruiting or vegetative growth of specific crops. There are many strong marks of these pre-mixed nutrients on the market, but other farmers consider themselves in considerable difficulties when attempting to utilize a handful of the "indoor plant foods" or other nutrients intended for soil or pre-fertilized plant mixture. These products are also not appropriate for hydroponics since they are not 'pure plant food.' A nutrient blend that is marketed for hydroponic usage and is a full-plant food is often preferred to be purchase.

To be 'complete,' a hydroponic nutrient needs to have the essential elements for plant growth, which are:

- Nitrogen (N)
- Potassium (K)
- Phosphorus (P)
- Calcium (Ca)
- Magnesium (Mg)
- Sulphur (S)
- Iron (Fe)
- Manganese (Mn)
- Copper (Cu)
- Zinc (Zn)
- Molybdate (Mo)
- Boron (B)
- Chlorine (Cl)

As there are no clear guidelines for doses, the amounts of these elements in your hydroponic nutrient continue to differ between labels. Any of the 'beneficial elements' of Nickel (Ni), Cobalt (Co), Silica (Si), or Selenium (Se) can also be present in other nutrients. Although these are not "necessary" (plants can still thrive without them), they can be beneficial to many crops.

Nutrient Problems

Either from different fertilizer salts or from purchasing a pre-made brand, issues can sometimes occur with deficiencies of one or more of the nutrients. The essential explanations for this are that

(1) the nutrient concentration may be too small, and the plants usually have inadequate nutrients.

(2) The mixture of nutrients you use may not be completely equilibrated, and one (or more) of the components may be deficient.

(3) Often, farmers may leave one of the fertilizer salts accidentally or use the incorrect fertilizer when the nutrient formula is weighted out. And when the remedy is well formulated, external and internal plant factors often prohibit the usage of some nutrients and signs of deficiency.

Signs of Deficiency

The plant needs mineral elements, which have its collection of 'deficiency signs and symptoms,' all of which can be recognized by growers.

Several of the signs are identical, but some are quite different, and the most significant gardening and hydroponic books can clarify these signals.

Shortly below are the defective symptoms of growing factor (these will differ greatly between plants based on the extent of the deficiency):

Deficiency Symptoms

Nitrogen (N): Plants are small; leaves appear to be light green-yellow, especially in older leaves. The undersides of the leaf and the stems may produce a purple coloration on tomato plants.

Phosphorus (P): Plants are typically shocked, and the color is dark gray. Older leaves initially have signs, and plant growth is still staggered. The shortage of phosphorus in certain plant species may be due to environments that may be too cold to absorb the nutrient, as opposed to a lack of phosphorus in the solution.

Potassium (K): The older leaves are yellowed, with dispersed dark (brown or black) marks, and tissue loss is observed. The plant is stunted by a serious deficiency, and any leaf may turn yellow and curled. On lettuce, the leaves may be yellowed and bronzed, beginning from the old leaf.

Sulfur: Sulfur deficiency is not typical–the leaves may be yellowing, first seen in the fresh growth.

Magnesium: Tomato crops with older leaves are usually defective in forming yellowed areas between veins that remain white.

Calcium: Young leaves are twisted, low in size, and with patched or necrotic (dead) regions before the older leaves. Bud growth is hindered, and root tips can die. Tip burn on lettuce is a sign of calcium deficiency, but certain causes not associated with a solution deficiency often cause it. The blue end of tomatoes is often induced by lack of calcium in the fruit tissue (not actually in the solution for nutrients), which becomes, under some environmental factors, something of a 'calcium transfer' concern in the vine.

Iron: The deficiency is specifically seen as yellowing of the fresh growth and younger leaves along with the green roots of the leaf (this separates them from the magnesium deficit first found on the older plants).

On crops like tomatoes, deficiency can occur when the conditions are too cold, rather than induce by a specific solution deficiency.

Chlorine: The deficiency reveals wilted leaves that grow yellowish and necrotic, and eventually turning bronze.

Roots become stunted and thickened near the tips.

Manganese: An interveinal yellowing on younger or older leaves based on the form of plant. Gray, dry areas can develop, and leaves may fall.

Boron: Plant size is usually reduced; the point of growth will die. Root tips are sometimes bloated and polished. The leaves are gradually thickened, brittle, and can be twisted with a yellow spot.

Zinc: Small plants of decreased length and leaf scale of the internode. Leaf edges may be twisted or ruffled, but even yellowing between the veins of the leaf may occur.

Copper: The deficiency is uncommon, but young leaves, sometimes with rusty, dry patches, may turn dark green or twisted.

Molybdenum: The older leaves grow interveinal yellowing and lead to the younger leaves. The leaf edges can cause the leaves to squirt or to cup.

Solution strength – under and overuse, measurement

The quantity or consistency of the solution has significant effects on plant growth and production, given that the product utilized is full and balanced. It is, therefore, essential that a valid unit of measure is used to quantify solution concentration. Many farmers may tend to operate with ppm using TDS meters, although the industry now standardizes the EC (electric conductivity) solution measuring tool, which is a reliable and practical way to track the nutrients. All TDS or ppm meters simply do is calculate the EC of the solution and then translate it to PPM using an approximate conversion figure. The problem is that this conversion figure is never quite precise since various nutrient solutions with different composition of nutrient components have different PPM values. The real reaction of the plant root system is the EC (or osmotic concentration) of the nutrient, and this is what should be calculated. There are a variety of EC meters (sometimes labeled CF), and farmers also use "waterproof" pen-style meters. Based on where you're in the world, the units displayed on the meter may be different, so it is simple to differentiate all EC units.

Microsiemens/cm (EC) or conductivity factor (CF) (depending on the nation in which you are located) are the most common units. Certain unit forms used or sometimes represented in crop recommendations are Millimhos, micromhos, and millisiemens (mS).

The conversion between all of these units is:

1 militiamen (EC) equals 1 millimhos, equals 1,000 microsiemens, equals 1,000 millimhos, equals 10 CF.

It is merely a case of moving the decimal position between the various units.

It is necessary to operate the right EC for your specific crop and method. Some vegetables like leaves and other greens require much less EC than fruit crops like tomatoes, and each crop has an ideal EC range of color for optimum production. When the EC is stable for a specific plant, it shows as noticeable signs throughout the field. A high EC essentially places plants under 'water stress' when the plant cells tend to drain oxygen, leading to the more condensed solution of nutrients that cover the roots. As a consequence, the first symptom of 'overuse' nutrients is the wilting of plants, even though an adequate nutrient solution is given. If high EC conditions are not really extreme, plants must adapt to these conditions, and you will see a 'strong' development, mostly darker green, with shorter plants and smaller leaves.

When the EC is small, the reverse occurs–more water is soaked up, development becomes sluggish and fluffy and sometimes tends to be greener.

The taste and consistency of the entire crop should decline–concerning the dry matter, shelf life, firmness, and color. As other variables, such as water intake from solution, a concentrate of nutrients during warm times, or nutrient intake, often influence EC, it is necessary to have EC assessed, tracked, and modified periodically under various environmental conditions.

The hydroponic solution can achieve optimal growth and yields by relying on the two most critical solutions, parameters-nutritional quality and nutritional concentration. If things go wrong, it is always crucial that you can accurately detect a deficiency symptom until it begins to have a significant impact on your crops. As always, carefully tracking your crop is the most reliable line of protection for growers from remedy issues.

LIGHTNING

In favor of saying 'yes' to plants, it is more appropriate to claim that the plants need light to grow, and at the same time, they need darkness. In hydroponics, we can now have all the energy we need to raise plants, but they don't require sunshine in this situation.

All plants always require is the Corleone dorm of light and the required volume of energy to reach their maximum potential.

Here, we can see what light plants require to grow, what artificial light does to remove sunlight and its failure, and why a mixture of both is the better option.

Why light impacts the development of plants

Light is essential, and you'll appreciate the importance of good light (especially sunlight) when you become a gardener. Apart from mushrooms and fungi, we can't produce much in the night. Learning light specifications are important for your plants and may have direct effects on your purse if you use artificial lighting tools.

Here, the basic elements of lighting conditions and the photosynthesis that plants need to develop to their maximum capacity are described.

-Photosynthesis

Here, a brief summary of the key factors of what hydroponics is all about.

Plants are labeled as autotrophs, and it ensures that they will build nutrients inside their bodies. To achieve so, they would collect the following from the atmosphere:

- Absorb minerals and nutrients through the rooting system
- Take up water through the rooting system
- Absorb carbon dioxide through the pores in the leaves

To combine all these for food, a plant requires energy, and this is obtained from light by the green chemistry in its leaves called Chlorophyll.

When carbon dioxide and water are combined with sunlight and chlorophyll, oxygen molecules and glucose are formed. In this situation, the glucose is required for the development of the plant and the fruit, and oxygen is emitted into the environment.

Seasonal Lighting Effects

The one big drawback of the sun is that it's not the same all year long. Throughout the different seasons, the duration and strength can shift. Plants have adjusted to this, and if in spring and summer, there is a lot of suns, the plants focus on developing and giving fruit and flowering.

Throughout the winter season, plants rely more on energy consumption and growth reduction. Photosynthesis is reduced, and the leaves tend to lack chlorophyll. Thus, we see leaves that are orange, yellow, or red during the fall.

Why is the Light Spectrum Important?

It is when things get fascinating, and it is possible to see the light, the signal to remove the amount of light the sun generates.

The visible light ranges between 390 and 700 nanometers in wavelength. The multiple wavelengths within this spectrum give the human eye-specific colors. The most widely recognized shades are ROYGBIV or Red, Orange, Yellow, Green, Blue, Indigo, and Violet. Blue contains the maximum duration and the lowest intensity, and blue and violet lights have shorter wavelengths and more power on the other end of the continuum.

The leaves on plants react to light falling into the wavelengths of 390–700 nanometers, where chlorophyll in the leaves consume light to grow food. Also, only one component of the spectrum is focused on plants, and the chlorophyll represents the green portion of the spectrum is 495–570 nm range, and thus the leaves are white.

Blue Light Spectrum

The light wavelength is 400–500 nm. It is energy-packed light, which affects the growth of leaves we know as 'vegetative' or 'veg' development. This blue light is caused by chlorophyll output and only limited quantities compared to red light are sufficient.

If there is not enough blue light on trees, they are softer and have yellow lines in the leaves rather than white.

Red Light Spectrum

This low energy portion of the continuum is vital for plants to flower and grow, so there would be sluggish or weak flowering if there are deficiencies in this range.

Farmers need to consider the range as it is up to them to substitute sunlight as they expand indoors, and from the next section, you can see that this is not as simple as it sounds.

Challenges of Replacing Sunlight with Grow Lights

All that can be observed as long as plants absorb the correct kind of light that spans the whole spectrum.

The three crucial factors are:

1. **Spectrum:** Both red and blue are required for plants to flourish.
2. **Intensity:** That is the luminosity of the sun, and how much energy falls on the leaf as photons. It determines the photosynthesis rate, and the greater the speed, the higher the photosynthesis output.

3. **Duration:** This is the amount of light a plant faces throughout the day. The seasonal light impacts plant development, such that shifts in these trends impact the overall plant production.

If we reproduce the sun with those lamps, all of the above must be reproducible. Among the three, time is the hardest to replicate as it just takes longer to control the lights.

Pressure may be a big problem when those through lights are used. Indeed, the result could change if the light is placed closer to the plants to improve the power. However, it could produce more heat, so the plants will continue to fall or to die.

The type of light used can also be challenging as the sun provides one source that generates the maximum spectrum of light through the different blue and red wavelengths. With artificial illumination, no light bulb or sole source is yet feasible to create all ends of the continuum and the blue and red ends of the continuum.

Indoor growers also use a combination of colder and warmer light sources to help them do this. It is not straightforward to start replicating sunlight, however when you strike the correct combination of several sources of light and a few checks and errors. In an indoor hydroponic device, farmers can produce excellent performance.

Common Grow Light Options

It is a short review of popular light options for growers indoors utilizing hydroponic systems indoors.

HID (High-Intensity Discharge): Such incandescent lights are growing indoor cultivation. They're hungry for power and put out a lot of fire. It ensures that you are only allowed to bring them next to the trees. The high-pressure sodium (red) and the metal halide (blue) are part of the HID eyes- it is more widely utilized for commercial hydroponic farms.

Fluorescent: These solutions for lighting are simpler to handle, produce less heat, and last longer while being cheaper to power. The only disadvantage is that they generate colder (bluer) light and do not meet all the needs of plants. Such a form of illumination is most commonly seen in DIY systems where it is paired with other red-spectrum light growth as it produces fruits or flowering plants. This kind of illumination is more than suitable for herbs. The most common variation is T5.

LED: Lights Emitting Diodes are increasing in popularity as both blue and red ends of the spectrum can be built to produce light. Such light sources should be used in the same lighting stand, meaning that light sources are not to be mixed or combined. These are the most cost-effective to manage for indoor growers.

Calculating Garden Lighting Needs

Now that lighting is crucial to plant production, we have to analyze how the quantity of light needed for a defined area, and some of the lighting styles can be determined.

It is crucial since lights can produce different quantities of energy, so introducing more or fewer of them to help plants grow is no remedy. If this can harm plants or hinder their development instead of supplying the appropriate amount of light they require, it is often essential in the procurement of a lighting device as they are both somewhat specific in service, purchasing costs, and operating costs. Another factor to remember is that any form of lighting produces specific quantities of light, and that may be important for the cultivation and overall safe plant development.

CHAPTER FIVE

LEARNING HOW TO BUILD YOUR OWN HYDROPONIC SYSTEM - FROM EASY TO MORE ADVANCED SET-UPS

1. THE KRATKY METHOD

This approach has been discovered by B.A. Kratky from Hawaii University. Kratky will basically be seen as the society of deep water, albeit without a generator.

Though Deep-Water Culture is a necessary and secure method of construction among the six forms of hydroponic systems, Kratky makes it much cheaper and more straightforward. It is because farmers do not need to purchase electronic equipment with Kratky, so they do not require power to operate. People claim you should create and "place and forget" a Kratky device. Plants are permitted to do their own stuff before the time of harvest. That's a little real - Kratky is a mostly passive device, no electricity is required and no pumps and no wick are used.

Growers don't have to adjust resources such as other processes in the reservoir. In principle, Kratky is also a low-maintenance device that can operate for weeks on its own.

How does it work?

As you know what plants are required for our evaluation of nutrients and hydroponic nutrients, plants ultimately need oxygen, water, and light to thrive. They need macronutrients and micronutrients to achieve their full potential growth.

All these plants are supported clearly by the Kratky method: nutrients are applied to the container/reservoir. Plants are put in a net pot of growing media (like hydroton, Rockwool) suspended over the surface. The roots of plants are partly submerged in water and exposed to air in section. People do so to ensure certain plants get sufficient water and oxygen.

If the plants grow, the amounts of the water decline as the plants absorb the water, creating a void between the roots open to the sun. The "air distance" is necessary because the plants breathe there.

It ensures that plants can also consume ample nutrients, water, and oxygen in times to come. If the water in the tank is almost zero for fast-growing crops, our plants may have reached their harvest date. You will add more water and nutrient solutions and test the pH level if you want the plants to continue developing.

Tools Needed

- A tub/tank. Depending on the scale of the plants and how big the Kratky network is. A milk jar often works if the cultivated plants are small. In the example, a black bucket of 5 gallons has been used.
- A table. A synthetic one fits well, or even styrofoam. The deck hugely significant, and it protects plants from rodents and pathogens and stops water from vaporizing in the tub. And above all, it protects the plants above the surface. If your tank has a cover, you don't have to buy another one. Yet you have to have one if it doesn't.
- Net pots. Again, choose the size you want. In the example, a 3-inch Hydro farm Net Cup has been used.
- Growing medium. We like Hydroton as its pH is neutral, and vigorous air aeration is simple to deal with.

- Hydroponic nutrient. In the example, the General Hydroponics Nutrient 3-part package has been used.
- Tools for pH calculation. The pH meter helps to test the system's pH level.

A tool for pH regulation. You should use the pH tool to test your system's pH level if it is too tiny or too large and change it accordingly.

How to set up a Kratky system

Step 1: Drill/cut the lid, creating a hole large enough to place and hold a net pot.

Step 2: Fill the reservoir with water (distilled or tap water is fine as long as it is not contaminated).

Step 3: Connect the hydroponic nutrients by the bottle at the recommended numbers. Remove from each Hydroponic container after filled with the air.

Step 4: Test the solution's pH degree with the pH meter. If 5.5-6.5 is true, the nutrient approach is the right one.

Step 5: Adjust the pH level with the pH kit if it drifts out of the suggested number at between 5.5 to 6.5.

Step 6: Place the net pot on a drilled lid with rising media and plants. Hold portions of the roots in the sun, and the rest fall into the solution of the nutrients.

What types of plants can you grow with Kratky Method?

The Kratky is ideally adapted to leafy greens, plants that develop rapidly, these contain vegetables, lettuce, and herbs.

You can also grow large plants like tomatoes or peppers, but a bigger container is required. To allow the exposure of the roots to water and oxygen as well, developing bigger plants may need more daily tests to ensure the water and nutrient level is 2-3 inches.

Potential Challenges and Downsides of the Kratky Method

Suitable for small plants

Particularly the leafy greens like kale, spinach. It does not work for fruits such as strawberries, peppers, cucumbers, and other hard areas.

Not built for larger systems

If you want a productive hydroponic garden that can impress your friends and provide your family with some vegetables, the Kratky device will do well. But a recirculation and electricity cycle is more realistic if you choose to grow it big, or generate food on a larger scale.

Pests

Kratky is a passive, silently operating machine. This may be a pleasant opportunity for rodents such as mosquitoes, crickets, mice, grasshoppers. It's just a normal response, just be careful to predict and cope with it.

Covering the container is important

That is why the deck plays a deciding role. It helps defend the environment from external threats such as plagues, rainwater, and temperature. Most people like to grow outdoors for full light. Make sure it doesn't attract rainwater into the tank. Too far, and the system's water level will rise, and plants will drown. In addition, the system's pH and ppm will subsequently alter. Have some sort of cover above the structure like a roof. But most plants will survive and prevent much of the rainwater from entering if they grow well. Best to put the machine indoors for heavy rains.

Take control of other factors

Kratky is not entirely hands-off, in fact. There are other factors you need to think about. Mix the nutrients thoroughly with high-quality water, and maintaining the pH of nutrient water at a satisfactory level for the initial setup is quite critical. Otherwise, you will periodically test and change them later. However, it is best to check the pH, water level, and ppm from time to time to ensure optimum growth for plants.

Nor will the temperature remain constant much of the time. Hold the device in areas where it is not adjusted easily. In the dry summer season, providing specific cooling methods helps.

Bottom Line

Even if you need a pump and the electricity to operate as in Deep Water Culture, Kratky shows that you can still develop plants passively (especially green vegs). The Kratky technique is an easy and calming way to pursue Hydroponics. If I suggest a simple program for beginners and kids that is quick to construct, Kratky would undoubtedly be one of them.

2. HAND-WATERED BUCKET

This very simplistic and quick to build the device is still simple and economical and will yield excellent results. The series of holes that ring the bucket is about 1 1/2" inch above the bottom. This allows a limited store of nutrient solution wiped from the capillary activity of the developing medium up to the plant roots.

Great for big plants, a single tomato or pepper plant can be easily treated or also just a few smaller plants, including salad or herbs. NOTE: You may need additional assistance for big plants to help hold the plant growing.

Materials Required

- **5 Gallon Bucket:** For this method, the Professor prefers a pure Perlite or Perlite/Vermiculite combination, although a significant number of the media do fit well.

- **Fiberglass Window Screen (Optional)** – A limited amount of window screen should be used to insert the overflow hole in the cover, which helps avoid the growing medium from dropping off.
- **Hydroponic fertilizer**: Hydroponic fertilizer of good quality is needed. Soil fertilizers contain no essential micro-nutrients.

- **pH Test Kit**: You need to test and change the pH of your nutrient solution. Quite important:

Note: Hydroponics and organics provide a low cost "Starter" pack consisting of standard hydroponic fertilizer (1-pint pH up, 1-pint pH down) and directions for the evaluation package (right for hundreds with tests) with two bottles of pH fluid (1-pint pH up).

ASSEMBLY OF SYSTEM

1. Drill a set of holes on top of the container in a New plastic bucket around 1 1/2" (4 cm). The number and measurements of the holes are not significant, typically 6 to 10 holes (3/8" or 1/2" in diameter) are appropriate. NOTE: Holes around 3/8" appear to be easy to cover up. The larger the void, the more possible it is that phase #2 is required. The large holes can dry out a growing medium quickly.

2. Optional: Place window screen over holes from inside the bucket. When you apply the growing medium, you can keep the screen or stick the screen together with a tiny amount of silicone coating. Wait for the treatment of silicone before applying medium to expand. NOTE: The screen just stops the growing medium from collapsing. You can skip this move if you don't like a little mess, or if your gaps are relatively small or if your can medium stays well together.

3. Remove the form from the container. NOTE: The growing medium needs to be washed and presoaked once used, depending on the type of the growing medium used.

Plant in the growing medium your seedling, root cutting, or seed. The Professor advises that you launch your seeds separately and only add the seedlings to your program.

CARE AND FEEDING INSTRUCTIONS

Hand Water Version

4. Blend the nutrient solution as per the fertilizer kit directions. Test the pH and react to it. The required pH

value differs according to plant requirements and the form of a growing medium.

5. The one-gallon milk jug is a simple way to blend the nutrient and add one gallon at a time. You will use another five-gallon bucket or acrylic tub (do not use glass containers. Otherwise, you can get algal) to blend more than one gallon at a time. If the proportions are combined at a time, the excess nutrient solution has to be aerated by an aquatic air pump and an air stone to keep it from stagnating. The bin for recycling will have a loosely fitted cover for the collection of waste.

6. Apply the pH-adjusted nutrient solution to the bucket gradually until you have an excess discharge from the leak troughs (approximately 10-15%).

If possible, repeat phase #6 periodically. It depends regardless on the conditions and the scale and form of the plant(s). It needs a little test and error to learn where and how much to drink.

Automated Version

7. Cover the tank with water and combine the nutrient solution as per the fertilizer kit directions. Test the pH and react to it. The required pH value differs according to plant requirements and the form of a growing medium. Place the drip line on the pump then bring the device into the holding tank. Link the pump to the timer. Set the timer and attach it to the outlet. NOTE: A quick cycle timer is expected to be configured for quick cycles. A temporary portable system from a home center would typically function because it can be completed within only one minute. A reasonable starting point for scheduling the timeout is once or twice a day for a minute.

Place the drop line on the base of the plant such that the nutrient solution flows out.

3. HYDROPONIC DRIP SYSTEM

When costs vary from location to location, the exact amount you receive in your particular region can be calculated. However, you can be a four-station drip device to develop broad plantings and purchase all the required materials for less than $100 - it is eventually possible to design this device for between 60 and 80 $. You may have some of the required materials around the house already. Since the device has been built to generate four plants in 5-gallon buckets, you can easily change it to cultivate more or fewer of your own plants, in containers and buckets that are larger or smaller.

Additional Items You'll Need to Grow the Plants

- Hydroponic Nutrients (any type, as long as they're designed for hydroponic plants).
- The general hydroponics pH research package (to check nutrient solution pH) fits well and is the cheapest way to go.

PH (pH up and pH down) Change the pH after you have checked it if appropriate.

In fact, you will be able to utilize the leftover hydroponic materials, the pH check package, pH adjusters, and that media in retail stores such as Home Depot, Lowe's Wal-Mart, Costco, Big Lots, Kmart, etc.

The pump for the pool was also from Lowe's. It was the most expensive aspect of the whole scheme. The pump was about $40, so you don't require a pump that big for this machine to do the job as it helps you to extend the device further. Make sure that every pump you use has a reversible tank if you don't want to build one to avoid waste.

The holes/bulkhead fittings are accessible in any size and form. These are found in all sorts of sectors, but most home improvement retailers carry them anywhere in the shop where they are likely to be placed in many locations. I had these in the Home Depot electrical department at $1.97, just next to the electricity source.

You may need to ensure that the end of the through-hole is continued (top without the threads and nozzles), so the type tube you are using matches. The above photos match within the tubing about 5/8 inch in diameter. If not, you should use two tube sizes and a tightening bolt. And, by cutting a medium tube (the size that matches the opening), push it onto the opening and move the smaller tube into the larger. If not, you should use a tiny quantity of waterproof adhesive between the two measurements and a hose lock to ensure it is safe. You can notice that an old garden pad suits well and may remove the vinyl pad for the return (drain) row.

The first move is to trace the thread and the nozzle side of the hole on the bottom of both 4-gallon buckets. You'll want the file to be close to the bottom of the container, but not so near that you can mount the filet on the nut (approximately one inch). That's why you can put it upright on a table or a bench, so most buckets are always balanced and don't fall over.

The spaces must not be too wide to prevent leakage. It will just be wide enough to hold the threaded side of the hole without a visible distance.

I use a rotary tool to make my own openings and a warm metal coat hanger. If you don't have one, you can quickly melt the plastic and then hack off some burs with a razor blade and make their edge clean.

Now that you have the whole break, plug the hole and pressure it. Just make sure you have the rubber gasket on the right-hand side, it is most definitely on the outside of the bucket and only the internal nozzle depending on the individual through holes.

In order to maintain the algae development down, it is essential to validate the containers. There are two items algae need to grow, food and light. Nutrients provide more calories, and the sun has to be screened.

Turn up the buckets and place tape over the opening (so you can't spray on them or in them). Offer the buckets a pair of black spray coats, or as many as required to cover all sun. Then as the black paint absorbs heat, give the buckets a few white spray coats. It represents light and helps keep the root zone temperatures dry. Make sure you paint just externally; the paint will not come in touch with the root or nutrient solution.

Placing the plants on the buckets is also quite easy, but just a few steps. Cut the filter component off the pipe first, then cut a section off to put it over the opening. This holds the fluid out of the conduit but also helps the water to drain out from the bottom quickly.

Furnace Filter

Now that the filter is in place, add a couple of rocks on it. I'd cover rocks to the bottom third. It preserves the tank and tends to remove water from the containers. The rocks often bring weight to the buckets such that they remain safely in place. They won't be able to push through heavy winds.

Note: Be sure that the rocks first are washed and sanitized by rinsing them off and soaking them for an hour, then rinsing them again. This decreases the risk of pathogens from soil and root diseases reaching the environment.

Growing Medium

Position the hydroponic solution on top of the rocks. Many materials may be used as a medium for growth, such as Grow Rock, Perlite, Vermiculite, etc. Any inert content (without nutrients) may be used. In this method, I particularly like and used coconut chips. Coco and coconut fiber are mostly the same thing, but coconut chips are still slightly larger. The greater partial size enables the root cell to absorb sufficient air/oxygen.

These coconut chips do have really extreme moisture, which is another factor I like to use them. This block cost $9.95, and all four buckets had plenty.

Watering and Drain lines

Now build a circle for all four buckets by using the vinyl tubing and a "T" attachment. It is the drippers that wash the pots. Once they have been made, take a paper clip and heat one, then place some holes in the ring with a flame of a candle.

Please note that I have only cut a little in the side of the buckets to keep the watering line snugly in place.

The feed line (watering) and the drain line layout depend on the design and the location of the buckets.

The feed line passes through a void in the center of the bowl. Then it is divided into two lines using a "T" connector, and each line is once again divided into two lines using the same "T" connectors. Divide one feed line into four different lines (three to each bucket).

Once precious nutrient water is injected through the top of plants, it then drops through the cubes and moisturizes the developing substrate (and roots) and flows back smoothly through holes on the bottom of the cubes into the reservoir. When all the Broccoli plant reservoirs have been built and developed in the Drip method, it can be re-circulated by the pump. The concrete bag is there to help bring weight to the table. From time to time, we have 50+ miles in an hour wind, so I have had an issue with the table or buckets that try to lift the rocks and the concrete bag off the table.

The reservoir

The tank component is also relatively simple: just paint the base and cover (outside) of the 18-30-gallon storage tote the way the buckets were created. Paint black, instead of white, to filter light and simulate light. When finished, slice the electric cord through the cover and force the pump in. You will then be able to launch your hydroponic device.

There are too many configurations you can do; there is no way to describe all of them. The seals may be mounted on a table, bed, wall, etc. So, you have to make sure that the tank is at least 6 inches below the containers. When not, the nitrogen solution can not quickly drain back into the tank.

The mechanism is simple; the pump pushes the solutions of nutrients to the top of the containers, where they leak through the seal and through the hole at the bottom. The return tube then pumps water back into the tank.

Drip loading and drainage line Setup

You may use various approaches on the return lines, but it will be a gentle slope back to the reservoir. You will see I linked the return lines with a "T" connection, from two containers, and then returned to the reservoir. PVC is not required at the end of the line heading back into the river, but it tends to prevent the fluid flowing much more. The tube which comes out of the side of the tank and coils through the middle of the table is the line which pumps the nutrient solution from the pump to water the plants from the top of the drip rings.

Water Cycling

I used this machine with a digital timer (I already had it), but later I bought another machine for $5.95 at Kmart with a specific model. It had a lot of settings and even a mask over the dial.

Make sure the device used for watering cycles is set at 15 amps (usually called high duty) for better performance with the device. I had one that had been approved for 10 watts, but in a few days, it burnt out. For about two years, the heavy-duty (15 amp) timers have not burned out.

You would probably want a timer with on/off pins right over the switch, not just a couple (for analog timers). There are several occasions during the day it would need to be switched on and off (to be discussed later). Digital clocks usually have several on/off cycles that can be programmed, so while a power loss is in operation, it can lose the memory because there is no battery backup.

Timer covered with plastic bags to keep it from getting wet in the rain

As you grow outdoors, you want to guarantee that the timepiece and cable ties are not damp or shortened. It can be achieved by keeping them in a position that is not damp, particularly though windy and heavy rains. In my situation, I warped three plastic sacks, one on top of the other (for tiny holes). The tube then securely fastened on the cables. It is not as spectacular as it should be, but the links held rain perfectly.

4. AQUARIUM HYDROPONICS RAFT

Materials you will need are:

- One piece of blue board foam!
- Uncooked beans!
- One fish tank or rubber made container
- (anything with a pump and clear sides)
- a ruler (or eyeball it) does not have to be perfect; the plants will not care!!
- One thin stiff piece, be imaginative to poke holes with! What it has to do is make space to fit in snugly with the seeds.

5. PVC NFT HYDROPONICS SYSTEM

Locate the hydroponic device in an enclosed building, such as an outside greenhouse or basement or a patio. The floor will be even so that the plants in the network equally absorb space and nutrients. Shield the system from hazards like a windshield when positioning the device outside and track the water levels more frequently due to water leakage due to evaporation. Take the hydroponic equipment inside during cold temperatures. When the device is installed in the interior of your building, install lights to offer extra illumination to the plants.

STEP 1: Assemble the Hydroponic System (Materials required)

The machine comprises of 6 growing tubings, consisting of a 6" PVC pipe, a PVC stand and trellis, a 50-gallon fertilizer tank, a pump, and a multi-tube tank. The tank lies under a table of 6" PVC growing pipes and is within the tank to transfer nutrients into a several smaller PVC pipes and plastic tubing to the plants. Each tubing has a drain pipe leading back to the tank. The funnel is placed on top of the pipes and delivers water to the pipes. The water is pumped into the plants in this method through a square of PVC, the pump, and then fired through tiny plastic tubes that flow through one of the larger tubes. The nutrient tubes comprise very small trout, one hole between the sites of the growing vine.

The nutrients dump the hole open and spray the roots of the plant. Around the same moment, the water jet jets the air such that the plants get ample oxygen.

STEP 2: Mix the Nutrients and Water in the Tank

Fill the 50-gallon water tank. Attach 2 cups of nutrients to the tank (or as the fertilizer label recommends), click on the pump and let the machine operate for around 30 minutes to combine all nutrients thoroughly.

STEP 3: Add Plants to the Growing Tubes

One of the simplest ways to plant a hydroponic garden is to use seedlings you have bought, particularly if you have little time to develop your seeds. The trick is to pick the healthiest plants you can find and extract all the soil from its roots. To clear the soil from the surface, immerse the root ball into a deep bucket of fresh water. Water too warm or too cold will shock the plant. Separate the roots softly to keep the dirt out. Any soil left on the roots may block the nutrient tubes with a tiny spray hole.

Once the roots are washed, drag as many roots as possible around the floor of the cup and then apply added clay caulk to keep the plant upright. The extended clay rock is heavy, but still very light so that the roots of the plant are not harmed.

STEP 4: Tie the Plants to the Trellis

Using the seedlings and cords to attach the plants to the trellis. The string will help them to climb straight up and optimize room in the restricted environment. Fasten the rope loosely on the top of the trellis, fasten on the base of each plant the clips and rope, and tightly loop the plant tips around the line.

STEP 5: Turn on the Pump and Monitor the System Daily

Check the water level daily; it might be appropriate to test it twice a day in certain areas, depending on the lack of water due to excess heat and evaporation. Every few days, check the pH and nutritional rates. You don't need a timer since the pump is working full time, just make sure the tank doesn't dry up so that the pump burns up.

STEP 6: Monitor Plant Growth

A few weeks after planting, the plants should cover the trellis completely, because they have all the water and nutrients they need to proliferate. It is critical that you keep a close eye on growing plants and tie or clip the stalks every few days.

STEP 7: Inspect for Pests and Diseases

Look for symptoms of threats and illnesses such as insect pests, chewed leaves, and foliar diseases. One diseased plant will easily invade all the others since they are too close together. Immediately kill any infected plants. Due to the absence of energy from hydroponic plants to find food, they may spend more time developing. It allows them to be healthier and better, as they will leverage some of this strength to fight diseases. Since plants' leaves rarely get soaked until it rains, leaf fungi, mildews, and mold are less likely to get damp.

Although hydroponic plants are excellent for battling diseases, pests do have to be combated. While hydroponic, insects and caterpillars may find a way into the greenhouse. Pick and uninstall any glitches you encounter.

6. DIY HYDROPONIC GROW BOX

Materials Needed

- Any size dark container bin (with lid). Use a size you've got the
- space for. I went with an 18 gal. Dark gray bin from Home Depot.
- A submersible pump. GPH depends on the size of the tub, and your PVC sprinkler system. I went with a Hydrofarm 250-GPH Submersible Pump
- PVC tank. I bought 1/2" long with one t-joint fitting and two end caps. Remember, this is a hydroponic DIY shell, so you can build it however you see fit.
- Heads of irrigation sprinkler. I picked up a 50 pack of 360o red amazon sprayers after Home Depot's five-pack struggled twice.

The proper drill taps for your sprinkler head.

- Net cups. Server cups. Volume depends on the depth of the container and the number of cups in use. For around 6-8 pots per container, I'd recommend the 2 to 3-inch cups.
- Clay (widening medium). You will find it at Amazon or your nearest growing store. The Aerogarden sponges are what I consider to function best.
- Flexible hose to attach the pump to PVC sprinkler system (dishwasher hoses work best)

Possible Materials

- Aquarium Air Pump with hoses, a one-way check valve, and an air stone.
- PVC pipe cutter
- Tape measure or a ruler
- PVC glue
- Epoxy
- Closet hanger "shelf" (holds the PVC tubing)

Step 1: Building Your Grow Box

After choosing your storage tank, determine the gap from the top of your PVC tube with sprinkler heads and net pot height. It is where we're going to put the hangers of the closet chain.

I have used a versatile knife for cutting plastic to stick to the rod holders with non-toxic epoxy/non-toxic hot glue. You should screw the hole in if you're confident, just try to plug the hole with stuff like water.

Step 2: Sprinkler System

Measure the internal bin width and then match your PVC tank. I consider the inner diameter of my bin to be 19″. The fittings were then measured: the t-joint was 23/4, each end cap was 21/4 long. I had my internal PVC duration by subtracting these sums to the total width and adding to eight (times per appropriate input).

Put a measurement together with all the components such that you have the right duration so that it falls perfectly into the container. Note: I noticed applying a lotion of hand to the ends that help check the ties without sticking together (I used some tiny hotel lotions for that). Mark the position of your sprinkler head, drill the pilot holes, and tap them with the right thread (usually supplied with your sprinkler head kit or at least specified so you can purchase the correct thread tap). Make sure that the t-joint points forward.

Step 3: Adding Oxygen (optional)

This move is not required because the sprinklers provide a ventilation effect. But I decided to install two air piers and a double aquarium air pump to deliver additional oxygen as the roots touch down, and the hydroponic device transforms into a hydroponic deep-water cultivation tub.

Place the bottom air-stone(s)- I have opted to pick them and push the tubes upside down. I drilled a tiny space to move the tubes in the top and make the top of the bin rest securely until it was sealed. Notice also the possible environment exclusion at the end.

Step 4: The Pump

Place the water pump on the base with the sprinkler cap and weigh the versatile pipe for attachment to the PVC sprinkler device.

Run out the top of the plug (I cut the bin and make the cord pass up and down so that the top can be flushed). Note the optional striping of the temperature.

Step 5: The Top

Now that the interfaces are full, we have to cut the top in order to attach nutrients and additional water to the net pots and an (optional) cover. I wanted to transform the net cups upside down and weigh the hole evenly spaced upside down. Since the top is plastic, a good kitchen knife makes it very easy to cut.

After I have cut the entry door, I have attached some electric tape to the bottom for the swinging door to reinforce. I then counted around the hatch and finished with seven potholes.

Step 6: Enjoy!

Go out now to bring your favorite herbs to vegetables into a greenhouse!

7. HYDROPONIC DRIP GARDEN FOR VEGETABLES, HERBS OR FLOWERS

How the System Works

In the black plastic tub, the hydroponic nutrients are processed. An inside-box water pump draws nutrients up to the falling lines and thus offers a nutrient solution for the growth of plants in the white plastic containers. The nutrients drain off the plastic pots that are then gathered by the yellow recessed deck on which the pots are set. Holes in the lid will pump the nutrients back into the black plastic shell. I have a timer that waters the plants for 15 minutes per hour on and twice more in the dark.

Hydroponic Systems; What is best for you?

Two simple hydroponic systems were used: Raft and Drip. Others include Ebb and Flow, Nutrient Video, Aeroponic, and Fog.

The raft device works by floating the plants on top of the nutrient solution. The nutrients are aerated by the air pump and air block. The raft method is perfect for lettuce development, but most plants survive best without the roots submerged in nutrients.

The drip mechanism functions just like plants are usually fed. Nutrients are supplied by gravity or a pump to the surface of the through water, which pulls more air into the water as the nutrients drain. This method will function well for virtually any plant form. This form is the downside of pump loss and clogged drip tubes.

The Ebb and Flow method is a common hydroponics program. The pots are put in a bathroom that is filled by a water pump with several inches of nutrients. The containers are filled from the bottom up. The water is turned off, and the pool flows back into the tank of nutrients after the pool has been filled. One of the drawbacks of this form of device is that it needs a huge tank to provide all the necessary resources to fill the bathroom and enough to hold it not dry. Like the drip system, you may even pump loss.

In the Nutrient Film method, the plant roots are put on a thin layer of streaming nutrients. As per my experience, these systems are challenging to build and not a suitable starting point for the hydroponic enthusiast.

The Aeroponic and Fog structures atomize the nutrients when suspended from the surface. It may be a very convenient approach to develop plants as the atomized solution provides a significant quantity of oxygen with which the roots survive. Many of the devices bought at home that are called "Aeroponic" are not aeroponic. Such home systems use tiny pumps and spray dumps to dust the bottom of net cups and roots.

The limited source pumps can not generate the sort of pressure required to atomize the nutrient solution such that the benefit over a drip or flux device is doubtful. I've stopped this because the tiny spray nozzles tend to obstruct more than the more significant drip emitters. Fog systems are very recent, and I do not know the durability or usability of hydroponic enthusiasts of such devices

Step 1: Materials Needed

Here are the items you will need:

- 1 - 27-gallon heavy-duty plastic storage box with recessed plastic lid
- 10' of 1/2" PVC pipe
- 5 - 90 deg PVC elbows
- 3 - PVC T connectors
- 1 - 3/4" to 1/2" PVC reducer
- 1 - 3/4" PCV pipe to 3/4" Male Thread connector
- 4 - 1/2" PVC J-Hook Hangers
- 1 - Male Quick Disconnect to male 3/4" hose thread
- 1 - Female Quick Disconnect to female 3/4" hose thread
- 1 - 1/2" hose barb to female 3/4" hose thread
- 1 - rubber washer with filter screen
- 3' of 1/2" flexible rubber hose
- 1 - Active Aqua PU160 water pump
- 12' 1/4' O.D. drip line hose.
- 12 - Drip stakes or drip nozzles with tie-down stakes

- 12 - Square Plastic pots sized to fit three across the top of tote lid
- 1 - 24 Hr timer with 15 minutes on/off timing intervals

The first 11 products on the list were all purchased from Home Depot and are popular in most hardware stores. The remaining were bought in a Billerica MA nearby hydroponics shop.

Tools Needed

- Miter box and miter saw or hack saw for cutting PVC
- Sandpaper, small round file, or deburring tool to deburr cut PVC
- PVC purple primer and cement adhesive
- Electric Drill with assorted bits
- 1" speed orbit or 1"-hole saw
- Awl or Nail to place drill starting mark in PVC
- Utility knife

Hydroponic Supplies Needed

- Your choice of hydroponic nutrients (I'm using Botanicare Pure Blend Pro)
- Your choice of growing media (I used about 15 liters of clay balls)

Step 2: Box Setup

The plastic box lid must be adequately sturdy for bearing the weight of the pots and plants without excessive bowing. The deck often has to be recessed to collect the nutrient solution as it flows from the containers. Flow troughs in the lid and lets the nutrients flow back into the shell. The bulk of big hardware stores can be contained in heavy-duty shipping boxes like this.

You want to choose square pots that are put flat in 3 around the plastic lid's recessed portion. You will also be able to get four pots around the length of the lid and 1" between half a dozen containers- the containers I have picked the match correctly. Compare from the top outside of the length of the lid upwards, two pots lined up side by side, and three pots lined up side by side.

Step 3: Cutting the PVC Pipe

Now take your 1/2" PVC pipe and cut the following pieces:

- 2 - The length of three pots + 1/4"
- 4 - The length of two pots + 1/4"
- 2 - one half the length of three pots - 3/4"
- 2 - 2" long pieces

I've used my inexpensive plastic miter box, and I've seen the PVC split. Without the miter box, you may use a hack saw, but I prefer how the miter box brings up the top—using any sandpaper, a small circular file, or deburring tool to extract plastic burrs from the cutting until all the parts have been removed. Make sure that after deburring, you blast out some loose plastic pieces as they will burst the drip lines.

Both the cut PVC pieces and PVC fittings should be put before installation in their final location.

Step 4: Drill Selection for Drip Line

Select a boiler bit of one size smaller than the actual drip line diameter (O.D.) My drip was 1/4" O.D., so I wanted a boiler bit of 7/32". Take 1/2" PVC (none of the parts you cut in the last step!) to the left and boil the PVC side hole with the 7/32" boiler. Remove some plastic burrs with a knife (don't injure yourself). Only cut on the surface because you don't want to adjust the diameter of the opening.

Take a tiny part of the conduit and sever the conduit ends at an angle of 45 degrees. Now start putting the end of the drip tube into the drilled spot. The opening is narrower than the conduit, and the tubes don't have to meet. If it slides in, you have to pick a smaller box part.

To bring the tube into the opening, I noticed that I was able to push a thumbnail with one hand against the tube, while I grasped the tube with the other hand and then pushed it back and forth. The inserted tube developed a good pressure suit, which does not leak. If the tube can't be inserted into it, attempt to soak about 1/4" of the drip tube end quickly in hot tap water. That should smooth the tube, which will make it simpler to install it. If you also can not bring the tube in, you may have to move up a drill scale.

Step 5: Drilling Drip Line Holes

Take the two largest lengths of tube (in my situation, 16 1/4") and put a label 1 1/2" on the one side of the two lengths. Make a second point farther down on the same side of a PVC tube, the same width of the top of one of the containers. Now render the third label down again the width of the top of one pot on the same side of the PVC pan. Now, use the two small PVC parts (7 5/8" parts in my case) and label the two ends of both pieces on one side. After you have made this position, locate one more label on the halfway point between the two endpoints. At this stage, a vice clamp might be helpful, so open the jaws slightly wider than the width of the PVC tube.

Step 6: Assemble PVC Sides

NOTE: Purple and PVC glue are used to connect PVC pipes on all PVC fittings. It's pretty easy if you haven't experienced this before. Read and observe the directions and protections on the bins.

Connect a 90 deg PVC elbow without boiling holes on each of the four mid-size bits. If the fittings have been mounted, let the cement cure for a few minutes before continuing.

Assemble one side a day. Make sure that the pitches will not straighten away from the working surface when mounting the first leg. Enable a few minutes to heal the joint. Then touch the long pipe with the second elbow. Press the whole installed package down on a smooth work surface while keeping the joint in place until it dries. All the elbows and the two open ends of the pipe will reach the working surface. It will allow if not all of them reach the final PVC assembly.

Using the same equipment for the remaining long boiler PVC pot for two other sections of the first set.

Step 7: Assemble PVC Middle

NOTE: Purple and PVC glue are used to connect PVC pipes on all PVC fittings. It's pretty easy, even if you haven't done this before. Read the directions and health warnings on the can and observe them.

Place one of the PCV T-fittings at the end of each of the shorter PVC holes tubing. Focus on the working surface with the T-fitting and the drill hole points straight up from the work surface. Repeat the process with boiler holes and second T-fitting with the other small PCV plug.

The second collection displays the direction of the two modules and has now been grouped by a third T-assembly. Remember that the PVC pipe holes are not as noticeable as they face the working floor. Apply the T-fitting to one of the small pipes mounted in the center. Make sure that the T-fitting is placed straight from the working surface down as the boxes face down to the work floor. Enable the joint to recover for a few minutes. Place the other end of the T-fitting on the remainder of the short tube. Press the whole installed package down on a smooth work surface while keeping the joint in place until it dries. The T-shapes at both ends will lay flat on the top of the work with the boilers facing the work.

Notice that all boiling holes face the surface of the job. Assemble one joint at a time and let the joint regenerate before it passes to the next joint. Until the cement dries, ensure that any piece is pushed down to hold the installed device stable. The PVC must be versatile enough to allow for the application of the first and cement until each rectangle is finished.

Step 8: Final PVC Assembly

NOTE: Purple and PVC glue are used to connect PVC pipes on all PVC fittings. It's pretty easy, even if you haven't done this before. Read and observe the directions and protections on the bins.

The direction of the final PVC fittings and the remaining 2" pipe parts is shown in the first illustration. The assembling sequence is of little significance. Just start at one end and move your way towards the other. When it is completed, it appears like the first package.

Step 9: Adding Drip Lines and Legs

Using a knife or scissors, remove 12-12" long drip tubing bits. Each of the ends of every tube will be removed at a 45-degree angle for placement through the PVC pins.

Place a drop pipe in each of the 12 holes in the same procedure as in step 4. In the first series, demonstrate a PVC assembly of drip pipes.

Step 10: Hose Assembly

Place the 1/2" tube beard in the 1/2" flexible tube and add it as instructed. When the 3/4" female hose end is trapped in a rubber washing machine, disconnect it and install a rubber washer with a filter screen, as seen in the second set up. A filter screen can serve to catch the particles capable of plugging the drop lines. You will test and clean the filter screen if required. To check a one-way valve, look at the end of the female's quick disconnection. When the other end of the fast break can not be reached, it comprises a one direction door. I was able to punch off the one-way valve with a regular screwdriver. The fourth setup displays the disabled one-way valve. The one-direction valve impedes nutrient distribution and is the easiest way to eliminate the valve.

Screw the female quick off the 3/4" PVC tube thread, as seen in the package.

Step 11: Drill Drain Holes in Lid and Install Pump

Use 1/8" of the drill to boil drain holes in the clock. You ought to get drain holes in the middle of the clock selling them because you are in the four corners of the fabric. Also, remember that the boil holes will be in the lowest channels of the cloak where the nutrients are pooling. I have drilled smaller holes rather than a few large holes, as this tends to prevent dropping into the box some primary content (such as growing media).

Remove some plastic burrs from the boiling with a machine knife.

Now pick the corner to remove the shaft and pump cable. Test to see whether the pump plug passes into the hole. If the opening is not properly expanded with a safety knife, then the pipe will go through. Use sandpaper, a thin triangular file along the edges of the opening such that it will not dig through the 1/2 hole or power line. Put the water pump into the lower down pump recess. Verify whether the pump pipe passes into the hole.

Step 12: Checking Operation

Place the PVC assembly on the plastic box lid and connect to the PVC end of the quick disassembly of the shaft portion. Now place the 12 pots within the two rectangles in the first setup.

Unplug the water pump into the big plastic tub, dump about 5-10 gallons of water. Do so by gradually pouring water into the top of the pots and having the water drip through the hole in the fabric into the plastic tub.

It is a successful measure for a steady draining of the cover. Raise the cap with the hose gently and test to ensure that the water pump is entirely under the water and fixed securely to the plastic bottom of the tub. Cover the deck again and attach the drip stakes or drip emitters gently at the ends of the drop shafts.

When no-drip stakes emitters are connected, you can discover that the pump can not pump adequate water to hold all drip lines going. Plugin the water pump to see the waterfalls from any drop line. Enable the pump to operate for half an hour and test that all lines work and that no water spills from any PVC or drip lines. Disable the watcr generator.

Step 13: Adding Grow Media and Drip Stakes

The pots I utilized have large spaces in the rim, meaning that the clay grows and falls out so that I cut a tiny piece of screen and put it into a growing pot's edge. Fill all the pots with your option of growing media. I used clay balls. Place the drop pile near the middle of the bowl, but on the closest bottom, where the drip line leaves PVC. Shorten the drip line to the proper length and add it to the drip pin, as seen in the second illustration.

The third setup demonstrates an alternate watering cycle with inline and finishing drop emitters and aboard. This way too, drip emitters are often harder to locate than drip stakes.

Step 14: Operating the System

You are set to grow your hydroponic greenhouse. Ignore the seeding guidelines for the different plant forms and media that you use. Note that the containers in this device are ideal for small to medium-sized plants. Most plants such as strawberries and beans and flowers will fit well. Instead, big plants like tomatoes require more room and larger container sizes in order to survive, and so these tiny containers are not a suitable means of development. Note that four pots may be removed to install a more substantial (approximately 4x) bowl. It will allow you to develop larger plants like tomatoes. All four drip tubes may be used to feed the large pot that offers plenty of nutrients.

Build two of these systems to enable the staging of the factory. One program may provide increasing nutrients for vegetative plants such as basil and spinach, which can be used for the flora during the initial vegetative process. The second mechanism will produce flowering and fruiting plant nutrients. Because both pots are the same size, it is simple for the two systems to switch.

8. EBB AND FLOW HYDROPONIC SYSTEM

In order to simplify this process, water and nutrients are flooded and drained into your growing media. It occurs regularly and is handled by an electronic timer.

The cycle completes itself with two phases. Water and nutrients flow into the growing regions during the flooding phase. It is achieved through a water pump. That amount of water is large enough to protect the plants ' roots. If kept for a time in a developing environment, the nutrient mix will then flow back into your reservoir.

To be sure that the water level does not start to rise and will not only flood the trees and overspill the sides of the house, but you will also have to provide an overflow outlet - which, enables the extra water to escape to the tank when the water flows through the room.

One feature of this device is that it is highly adaptable to that room. The flood bed may be of any scale, as long as it is sufficient to accommodate the plants and pots while having plenty of room. Another element of size would be the grow lights, which will be enough to cover the whole room.

Parts and Materials Required

- Before looking at the appropriate parts, the flood trays should be listed. Since these come of varying quantities, you have to understand the width. As they flood, the water volume has to rise sufficiently to wash through the plant's roots, ensuring that there is no runoff.
- Be sure to focus the pot sizes on the width of your flood table while ordering. If they are too big, and the roots of the plants don't go to the bottom of the bowl, they can't take enough water and nutrients.
- 1 x flood tray of a suitable size – black is the best color.
- 1 x submersible water pump
- 1 x air pump – optional, you don't need this, but more oxygen is always a good thing.
- 1 x digital or analog timer which covers 24-hours
- 20ft x 1/2 Black tube – this is way more than you need, but probably the least you can purchase.
- Overflow and inlet fittings – Many growers make their own, but these Ebb & Flow Fitting Kits are super cheap and can make things far more comfortable to work with.
- 1 x reservoir tank – opaque to deter algae growth

When it comes to sizing your water reservoir, you need to know the following:

Before looking at the appropriate parts, the flood trays should be listed. Since these come of varying quantities, you have to understand the width. As they flood, the water volume has to rise sufficiently to wash through the plant's roots, ensuring that there is no runoff.

Be sure to focus the pot sizes on the width of your flood table while ordering. If they are too big, and the roots of the plants don't go to the bottom of the bowl, they can't take enough water and nutrients.

Note: You may need to flood the tank higher depending on the growing medium used. Most suitable kits have an extension to make this simple. In fact, every flood table over 4 ft square requires 3/4-inch fittings. This will suit your tubing and also your water pump's connection.

Assembling a Flood and Drain System

One of the most challenging aspects of designing a flood and drain system is ensuring that you have a sufficient foundation to house your tank. Some farmers use pond liners and build their own fields, but an old table or anything similar would be appropriate for new growers.

It should allow the flood table to sit above your nutrient tank. Once you have your support, you can follow these steps to construct the system.

1. Drill two 35 mm holes in the lower portion of the tray in the flood cover, this will be a few centimeters separated.

You will always be at one end of the tray because you have to move over the help bottom.

2. Screw both fittings into the flood tray. The rubber seal will be within your flood tray, while the end of the tube stays from outside.

3. Attach two to three extensions of Ebb and Flow into one of the bits you have already added to the bottom of your tray.

4. Place one of the panel fittings at the end. You've installed your overflow tray now. (You will need to change according to the size of the pot)

5. Place a screen on the rest of the portion at the bottom of the flood panel. It is the water source from your submersible pump.

6. Place the flood tray, so the fittings hang above the hydroponic reservoir.

7. You ought to weigh piping from the bottom of your tank to the fastener that supports the pipe on your flood shield. One thing to remember is that there will be a cover on your tank, and you have to cut holes large enough for both tubes to pass through. Each light in your nutrients will help the growth of bacteria.

8. Attach the tube to the water pump and attach it to the inlet link via the roof.

9. Add the tube to the overflow for a shorter duration; it lies within the cap and covers the water rim. It assists with the oxygenation as the water falls back into the tank.

10. Load the appropriate water in your tank and operate the machine—test for leakage either from the inlet or from the runoff.

11. You can then install your timer, and get ready for your pots or Rockwool cubes to be added.

When you choose an air pump, just make sure that you use black tubing, so your tank cover hole is tiny enough just to allow the tube to go through without illumination.

It is best to wait until you have your flood table while you are searching for a water pump if you want a 4 ft. X 4 ft. A 170 GPH (Gallon per hour) pump is ideal for the flood level. If your flood table is 4 ft. X 8 ft., it should allow a 300 GPH water pump.

Suitable flood and drain system growing mediums

Since flood rates can change when utilizing various growing mediums, it is essential to know which mediums are accessible to you.

- Rockwool – these are suitable when they are in both Rockwool blocks and also when cubes are used in pots.
- Coco Coir – This coco fiber is suitable to be used in both pots or in blocks.

Hydroton clay cake is the perfect medium for use in net pans. It should be remembered that it does not retain water as well, and the flood levels are higher.

Flood Cycle Times for Different Growing Mediums

Because each growing medium absorbs specific water volumes from the flood cycle, these periods can vary considerably. The flood and drain period periods are calculated here.

Multiple variables may be used to reduce or prolong this time. Both plant types and environmental factors may have a significant effect on the drying out of growing mediums. These times will be a strong starting point for scheduling your timer.

Hydroton pebbles

- It includes frequent flood cycles. Although they do not provide as much moisture as other growing mediums, they are incredibly common because they provide strong support for plants. In this growing medium, the most commonly followed cycles are:
- 15 minutes on – 15 minutes off
- 15 minutes on – 30 minutes off
- 15 minutes on – 45 minutes off

You will need to do some testing to make sure your Hydroton hasn't totally dried out before the pump timer starts again.

Rockwool

The Rockwool periods will vary from 3 to 5 hours. The plant size and weather in your growing region would have an impact on this process. The flooding time would generally remain the same for 15 minutes, but the nutrient period does not change. The easiest way to tell is to operate the program and drop the blocks every hour. When the block feels warm, and there is no falling humidity, then the next flood process is about to take place. It will change as the plants grow and absorb more water and more nutrients.

Coco

This growing medium will have the most considerable vector flood period because it dries out quickly. To figure out, you need to see how quickly the top 1/2-inch dries. You can see that clearly as the film is darkened from a dark brown to a light brown as it dries. When you use Boss Blocks, the flood period can be about 3–4 hours, depending on the setting.

Ebb and Flow Advantages and Disadvantages

Advantages

- Low Cost–This is one of the most inexpensive systems you can create. There are many parts you can improvise. Tanks and flood trays can be made from something of the correct scale.
- Simple to create–Ebb and Flow are really quick to construct. If your flood tray has little help, drilling the opening in and out of your inlet and overflow tubes is the worst part.
- Many Resources–the operation of the network means that all plants obtain adequate resources and oxygen. The flood should deter so much water, meaning plants can't suffocate.
- Ease of use – When the system is running, you have done all the hard work, and all you need to do is maintain your nutrients at the correct levels and give your plants sufficient light.

Disadvantages

Unstable pH levels – If your system fails in some region or you introduce so many nutrients/water, your pH will be taken out of the optimal range. If you have extra nutrients and the EC rates rise, you will also induce nutrient burns, and salts can build up in your system. Overflow can avoid so much stagnant water, and plants won't suffocate.

Breakdowns – Your water pump is the main point of failure. If this does not happen, then you just have to continue the next flood process before the plants start to die. Hydroton pebbles would be the first to fail as Rockwool offers you the most energy. A manual filling will be a quick repair, but the pump may need to be replaced.

Best Plants to Grow in an Ebb and Flow System

While you may develop several items in a flush and flux method, there are three types of vegetables that really perform well. These are often available in various strains, so you can have a little variety rather than growing the same.

Cucumbers

There are plenty of cucumber varieties that are ideal for an ebb and flow system:

- Mini cocktail cucumbers – This is collected at a length of around 2-3 cm.
- American Slicer type – These fruits are ready for harvest at a duration of 7 to 8 inches. They are often disease tolerant and grow very strongly in a hydroponic environment.
- Dutch type (seedless) – This form is famous because it offers the most abundant fruit of about 14 centimeters long. They've got thin hides with no sour aftertaste. This form of cucumber is also powdery mildew resistant, which may impact other varieties.

Lettuce

It is one of the most popular vegetables to grow in any hydroponic system. However, several varieties excel in these conditions. Here are well-proven high-performers.

- Salanova – This range is one of the latest fashionable salads and a perfect way to please friends and relatives. The only thing about this salad is that it develops small eyes, both standardized in shape and scale. Seeds that deliver different colorful salads may be purchased, but this variety is a little more costly.
- Green Butter – This form of salad is suitable for climates like Florida. It is solid enough to smooth out the mildew and sluggish to fire. It is an extremely efficient product and yields reliably.
- Green Frilled – This form of a salad may be suitable for colder climates because it is very resistant to heat. It provides a lot of flavor from its medium-sized heads. This type develops slower than other varieties.

Tomatoes

These may need support as they grow, but an ebb and flow system are ideal for this as everything will be stationary. The best two types of tomatoes to produce are:

- Cherry Tomatoes – Few varieties of cherry tomatoes are available (Sakura and Favorita) and are suitable for ebb and flow systems. Both styles are disease tolerant, though not susceptible to cracks or skin splits.

- Beefsteak Tomatoes – Geronimo and Trust are two of the most common commercial varieties. It is ideal for growing in an ebb and flow system since it grows immense fruits and is immune to diseases. These hybrid varieties need a lot of potassium when their fruit starts to grow, and these are certainly going to require help.

- Beefsteak Tomatoes – Geronimo and Trust are two of the most common commercial varieties. It is ideal for growing in an ebb and flow system since it grows immense fruits and is immune to diseases. These hybrid varieties need a lot of potassium when their fruit starts to grow, and these are certainly going to require help.

CONCLUSION

Hydroponics is a type of soil cultivation where plants are grown with or without an artificial medium in nutrient solutions. The cultivation is extremely productive and it conserves water and nutrients. Therefore, it is environmentally friendly.

Hydroponics is high tech, but only primary agricultural skills are needed. Air and root temperatures must be controlled, including light, water, plant nutrients, and severe weather.

In addition, hydroponic systems also often have to run in temperature-controlled settings such as greenhouses. It is indispensable to be mindful of the greenhouse conditions because hydroponics would no longer be economical to you.

There is no supportive habitat for plant roots in liquid hydroponic systems. It is also known as a solution culture; static solution culture, continuous-flow solution culture, and aeroponics are the three primary forms of solution culture.

In the former, plants are produced in hydroponic solution tanks. These are typically applications at home where hydroponic systems operate in glass bottles, plastic containers, tubes, and reservoirs. The water is also often aerated but sometimes unaerated, such that the ph of the water is small enough to enable the roots to have exposure to a daily supply of oxygen. The nutrient solution is changed, normally once a week, according to a preset timetable.

The continuous-flow solution culture is structured slightly, and the hydroponic nutrient solution runs through the surface. A common variant of this culture is the nutrient film technique; here, a very shallow stream of water containing all the dissolved nutrients required for plant growth is recirculated. A watertight root pad traverses the hydroponic nutrient solution in the lower half of the roots while the upper parts of the roots are exposed to sunlight and are supplied with sufficient supplies of oxygen.

Nevertheless, hydroponic aggregates are supported by a good natural or artificial source. The hydroponic systems can also be used where the nutrient solution is provided to the plant roots and not reused or capped in order to restore, refill, and recycle the surplus water.

The crop has very different requirements, and, as with any farming system, hydroponics would take care of the particular needs of each field. Hydroponic systems advance quickly today, and their yields are expanding numerously, achieving heights that we have never anticipated. Hydroponics is feasible in places not prone to standard cultivation, including deserts and space stations. People in densely populated areas may use hydroponics to cultivate their own fresh vegetables in rooftop gardens or walls. To conclude, hydroponic plants often grow more rapidly and are mostly free of soil-borne diseases.

Thank you again for buying this book!

Do Not Go Yet; One Last Thing To Do

If you enjoyed this book or found it useful, I'd be very grateful if you'd post a short review on Amazon. Your support does make a difference, and I read all the reviews personally so I can get your feedback and make this book even better.

THANK YOU, AND GOOD LUCK!

9 798643 426332